CIM Companion:

introductory certificate in marketing

Elizabeth Hill

Terry O'Sullivan

CIM Publishing

CIM Publishing

The Chartered Institute of Marketing
Moor Hall
Cookham
Berkshire
SL6 9QH

www.cim.co.uk

First published 2001
Revised edition 2004
© CIM Publishing 2004

Series Editors: John Ling and Mark Stuart

British Library Cataloguing in Publication Data
A CIP catalogue record for this book can be obtained from the British Library.

ISBN 0 902130 73 0

It is the publisher's policy to use paper manufactured from sustainable forests.

Printed and bound by The Cromwell Press, Trowbridge, Wiltshire.
Cover design by Marie-Claire Bonhommet.

The Chartered
Institute of Marketing

For Archie McLellan
1942-2000

contents

Study guide

This Companion is written to complement the recommended course text by Elizabeth Hill and Terry O'Sullivan, *Foundation Marketing,* 3rd Edition (2004), published by FT/Prentice Hall. It aims to offer you support as either an individual or group learner as you set off on the road to becoming a competent and proficient marketer. This is a process of learning that has two important elements:

Understanding marketing concepts and their application

The study text in the following Sessions has been deliberately written to highlight the foundation-level concepts that you will need to grasp as you begin to understand what marketing is, what it can achieve, and how it is implemented. The material is described briefly and concisely to enable you to cover a range of key material at an introductory level. It does not attempt to be comprehensive, and indeed, you should read widely from other sources, including the recommended course text (readings are specified for each of the Sessions in this book), the marketing press and national newspapers, to develop your understanding of the concepts introduced here. More comprehensive marketing textbooks may be useful too, as they provide a wider context for the concepts explained in this Companion, and provide more case studies and examples to illustrate marketing in practice.

Developing the skills to implement marketing activity

Equally important in the journey towards marketing excellence is the acquisition, development and refining of a range of skills that are required on a daily basis by marketers across all industries and sectors. These transferable skills hold the key to the effective implementation of the marketing techniques explored in the study text. The focus of the practical exercises in this book is on six key skills:

- **Communications** (e.g. report writing and making presentations).
- **Application of numbers** (e.g. data analysis and arithmetic).
- **Information Technology** (e.g. using the Internet, word processing, spreadsheets and presentation software).
- **Working with others** (e.g. group work, delegation and chairmanship).
- **Improving own learning and performance** (e.g. research and study skills).
- **Problem solving** (e.g. case studies).

The Sessions all contain six key skills exercises, each of which has been specially designed to enable you to practise your skills relating to some of the marketing concepts covered in that Session. By working through these exercises you will acquire and develop some of the most important skills that you will need as a marketer. Tempting though it may be to ignore the exercises and save time by simply reading the text, always remember the old adage, 'I hear and I forget, I see and I remember, I do and I understand'.

Other features of this Companion include:

- **Learning outcomes:** a set of objectives you can set for your learning in each Session.

- **Glossary of terms:** important definitions that are referred to in the study text.

- **Multiple-choice questions:** test yourself as to how well you have understood and can apply the concepts covered in the study text.

- **Discussion points:** food for thought that can be explored with others.

Key skills

The Activities interspersed throughout each Session have been developed in order to give students the opportunity to develop their knowledge and understanding of the issues raised. They also offer the additional benefit of each being focused on one of the six key skills: communication, application of numbers, information technology, working with others, improving own learning and performance and problem solving. We hope that they will be useful for any candidates working towards awards in these areas, as well as allowing students to develop relevant professional skills for marketing and marketing-related work. The following matrix indicates which Session Activities are targeted at which key skills.

	Communication	Application of numbers	Information Technology	Working with others	Improving own learning and performance	Problem solving
Session 1	1.1 Marketing marketing	1.5 The best laid plans...	1.3 Marketing orientation?	1.2 Loyalty check	1.4 Marketing myopia	1.6 Levi's
Session 2	2.4 Insulting the customer?	2.2 Don't stop the music...	2.1 Statistics.gov	2.3 Access all areas	2.5 Webbed feat	2.6 Who's online?
Session 3	3.5 Engine manual	3.2 Profit profiles	3.3 Site inspection	3.1 Soft furnishings	3.4 Be a better Internetter	3.6 Grocery mosaic
Session 4	4.4 A qualitative proposal	4.2 Driving forward	4.1 New cars by region	4.3 Designing a depth interview	4.5 Researching research	4.6 Marks & Spencer
Session 5	5.4 Many happy returns?	5.1 Terrific tariffs	5.3 Just the ticket	5.2 Class act	5.5 Guard your card	5.6 Sunny Delight
Session 6	6.3 Tween spirit	6.4 Give us a clue	6.5 Poor students?	6.1 Classic segments	6.2 From little acorns...	6.6 Organic and functional foods
Session 7	7.1 The benefit in question	7.5 Value for money	7.2 Design matters	7.3 A new lease of life?	7.4 Mind mapping product	7.6 Scrabbling for success
Session 8	8.3 Sounds profitable?	8.4 Elasticity exercise	8.5 What if?	8.1 What's it worth?	8.2 Picturing price	8.6 Currying favour?
Session 9	9.2 Channel vision	9.5 How much is enough?	9.3 Virtual retailing	9.1 On a role?	9.4 Service distribution	9.6 Grocer-e shopping hits a snag
Session 10	10.1 Colourful advertising	10.2 Campaign costs	10.3 Pocket-money profits	10.5 Ambient ambitions	10.4 Extending AIDA	10.6 Dome and gloom?
Session 11	11.4 Growing success	11.3 The right price?	11.5 Good form	11.1 Mystery shoppers	11.2 Customer scorecard	11.6 AOL in the UK
Session 12	12.5 The write impression	12.4 Currency conundrum	12.1 Being charitable	12.3 On the retail trail	12.2 International understanding	12.6 Blowing the dust off museums

Session 1

What is marketing, and why is it important to plan?

This Session will help you get to grips with just what marketing is and why it has become such an important function for all types of organisation. It will also outline the steps you will need to take when you start to plan an organisation's marketing activity.

LEARNING OUTCOMES

At the end of this Session you should be able to:

- Define marketing.

- Explain why a marketing orientation can help an organisation achieve its goals.

- Give examples of organisations that do and do not appear to be marketing orientated.

- Justify the use of a marketing plan as a management tool.

STUDY TEXT

If you were to ask a few people in the street what they think marketing is, chances are you'd be told it's about "selling", or "questionnaires" or "advertising", because this is the very public face of marketing activity – some of the techniques that marketers use to communicate with their customers and potential customers. But important though these techniques are, they by no means represent the whole meaning of marketing.

What is "marketing"?

Ask some marketing practitioners what they think marketing is, and the one thing they are likely to agree on is that **CUSTOMERS** are at the heart of marketing, because marketing is the business function that attempts to build mutually beneficial relationships between organisations and their customers and potential customers.

A wide range of definitions of marketing have been written over the years, but the one thing they tend to have in common is the emphasis on keeping customers happy. The Chartered Institute of Marketing defines marketing as...

'The management process responsible for identifying, anticipating and satisfying customer requirements profitably.'

Breaking this definition down a little, we can see how marketing activity works in practice.

... management process ... marketing activity is implicit in the management of a business. Sole traders, charities, retailers and international corporations all have to know who their customers and potential customers are, and what they must do to attract and keep those customers. Bigger organisations tend to have departments and members of staff with the title of "marketing" attached to them; smaller organisations often don't. But chances are, whenever an organisation is involved in conducting transactions with customers, it is "doing marketing", whether it recognises it or not.

... identifying and anticipating customer requirements ... the key to successful marketing is **customer orientation** – understanding the needs and wants of those customers and potential customers. Consequently, market research is one of the most valuable tools available to a marketer. Conducted either formally (using surveys for example) or informally (by simply talking to customers), research can provide revealing insights into what customers like and dislike, putting the organisation in the best possible position to provide what their customers really want.

... satisfying customer requirements ... when they understand who their customers and potential customers are and what they want, marketers are in a position to decide what sort of goods or services to sell them. They can also make decisions about how much to charge for these goods and services, how to let people know they exist and find out more about them, and how to make them easily available for people to buy. These are the key decisions that marketers have to make if they are to create and keep satisfied customers.

... profitably ... for organisations operating in the commercial business world, the purpose of conducting the marketing activity described above is usually very simple: to make a profit. The whole reason for attempting to satisfy customer requirements is to generate revenues that outweigh the costs of providing the desired goods and services. But profit isn't the only motive for marketing activity, and some organisations have other goals, which may also be achieved through marketing activity. For some charitable organisations drumming up support for their cause is just as important as raising money.

Activity 1.1 Marketing marketing

Prepare a PowerPoint presentation aimed at either a) a class of seven-year-olds or b) a meeting of your local Women's Institute or c) the Chamber of Commerce in your area, to explain to them what marketing is.

What is "relationship marketing"?

As the discipline of marketing has developed over the years, it has been suggested that the traditional definition of marketing given above is somewhat limited in its aspirations. The process of 'identifying, anticipating and satisfying customer requirements profitably' is certainly a good starting point, but it is equally important that the customers whose needs are satisfied when they buy a product from us are then encouraged to revisit our organisation time and time again. The concept of "relationship marketing" has been introduced to reflect the importance of organisations focusing on keeping loyal customers for the long term, not just engaging in a series of short-term transactions with them.

'The relationship marketing approach focuses on maximising the lifetime value of desirable customers and customer segments.' Payne, A. et al (1998), *Relationship Marketing for Competitive Advantage,* CIM/Butterworth-Heinemann.

Consequently, organisations that adopt the concept of relationship marketing tend to focus primarily on marketing practices designed to keep customers loyal, and make considerable use of one-to-one techniques such as database marketing to keep in touch with those who buy from them.

Activity 1.2 Loyalty check

Loyalty schemes are one way in which retailers attempt to build better relationships with customers. But are they effective? Or is it good ol' fashioned customer service, brand image, convenience and product availability that keep you happy? List all the retailer loyalty cards that are held by you and the others in your group. Now list the range of different benefits offered by each retailer. Which benefits are most likely to keep you returning to the same store time and time again? What other factors might encourage you to shop there (or discourage you)? Are your answers the same as the others in your group? If not, account for the differences in your opinions.

What is "societal marketing"?

Traditional definitions of marketing concentrate on the importance to an organisation of satisfying the needs of individuals, on the basis that keeping individuals happy is in their own best interests! Normally, if the individual's needs are satisfied, then the interests of society as a whole are being met too. Improved customer satisfaction leads to higher standards of living and quality of life. Thus the "societal marketing" concept is adopted by many organisations.

'The societal marketing concept holds that the organisation should deliver the desired satisfactions more effectively and efficiently than competitors in a way that maintains or improves the consumer's and the society's well-being.' Kotler, P. et al (1996), *Principles of Marketing* (European Edition), FT/ Prentice Hall.

Figure 1.1

There are circumstances, however, under which the best interests of an individual may be at odds with the best interests of society as a whole, and under such circumstances the organisation has to make ethical decisions about its activities. Organisations which sell products that pollute the environment, that exploit cheap labour in less developed countries or that have long-term detrimental health implications for their users might argue that it is the role of governments, not businesses, to uphold the interests of society as a whole, and that their responsibility ends with the satisfaction of their customers.

What is "marketing orientation"?

Most of us can name organisations that seem to put their customers first. We've all had experiences of exceptional customer service, when an organisation has made great efforts to leave us with that warm feeling of being very important to them. Sadly most of us have also had the opposite experience too. The impression that an organisation leaves with its customers generally depends on the extent to which it is "marketing oriented", or whether it adheres to another business philosophy.

Organisations with a **"marketing orientation"** recognise the importance of placing the needs of customers at the heart of their businesses, and believe that 'identifying, anticipating and satisfying customer requirements' is the quickest and most effective way of achieving their long-term goals. However, other organisations take a different view.

Those with a **"production orientation"** believe that producing ever larger quantities of identical products is the most effective business strategy, as this leads to cost savings through **economies of scale.** Indeed, in some industries, the more you produce, the lower the cost per unit, so economies of scale mean that firms can afford to undercut their competitors. Alternatively, if they don't reduce their prices, they will generate a higher profit margin on each item sold. In practice however, it's rare that all the potential customers for a particular type of product want identical things, so a focus on ever-higher production levels can leave a gap in the market that competitors can fill. So although the efficiencies that can be gained from production orientation might create opportunities in the short term, they seldom help the organisation achieve long-term success.

Those with a **"product orientation"** tend to focus on the technical capabilities of their products, and put all their efforts into improving these, whether or not the customers actually want better product features or facilities. This poses the real danger of missing out on major shifts in customer demands. There's not much point in improving the technology of a product such as a Video Cassette Recorder (VCR), for example, if the world has been convinced of the benefits of DVD, and is aiming to replace its VCRs as soon as it can afford to!

Those with a **"sales orientation"** are keen to sell their products to anyone who can be persuaded to buy them, regardless of whether the prospective purchaser has any need for the product. This means that, in the short term, they can generate good levels of sales. But in the long term, if the customer has no need for the product, or the product fails to live up to its claims, there will be no repeat purchase, no word-of-mouth recommendation from customers to potential new customers, and worse still, the customer may tell a dozen or more friends or colleagues about their dissatisfaction!

Activity 1.3 Marketing orientation?

Select a company whose product or service you are familiar with and that you consider excellent. Look at this company's web site and identify the features of the web site that suggest whether or not it is marketing orientated. Repeat the exercise for a company whose product or service you consider to be very poor. List the main differences between the two. To what extent are web sites indicative of marketing orientation?

Why has marketing grown in importance?

The fact that more and more organisations across the world are recognising the importance of the function of marketing can be attributed to a number of changes in the economic, business and social environment in which firms operate.

Competition

New sources of competition are continually entering the markets for many goods and services. The Internet, for example, is facilitating the growth of international competition, making it possible for new and existing businesses to reach a global market through their web sites. As competition grows, recognising any remaining gaps in the market, and filling those gaps, becomes harder, and only those organisations that consciously attempt to "identify and anticipate" customer needs have much chance of getting a sustainable foothold in a market.

Complex customer needs

In subsistence economies, where people struggle to buy enough to eat or find a home for their families, it is relatively easy to predict the needs of the market. These needs will simply reflect the physical needs of the human body for food and shelter. But in societies that are economically more developed, the needs of the market will reflect the people's psychology as much, if not more, than their physiology. Psychological needs, however, are personal and individual, and therefore are more difficult to "identify and anticipate" than physical ones.

Consequently, as economic prosperity across the world grows, so does the importance of a marketing orientation.

Supply chains

As businesses become more and more international in their operations, they are more likely to become dependent on other businesses to distribute their goods and services to their ultimate customers. When this occurs, they become dependent upon these third parties to translate and convey the needs expressed by the market to them, and lose contact with the people who ultimately buy the goods they sell. Consequently, it is even more important that they take seriously the task of attempting to identify and anticipate customer needs.

Complex organisations

In a large retailing business, the staff who are in the best position to listen to customers and make recommendations about the goods and services that would suit them best are the sales assistants. But these are likely to be among the most junior staff in the whole organisation, and the people who make the decisions about what to stock, how to lay out the store, or how much to charge, may well be located at Head Office. Under circumstances such as these, a marketing orientation becomes vital, as the decision makers need to find a way of harnessing the front-line information, and using it to determine the most appropriate policies for their businesses.

Environmental change

When countries' political situations change, when social trends gather momentum, when levels of economic prosperity change or the world is exposed to ground-breaking technological developments, customers needs and desires change with them. Turbulent times lead to turbulent markets, and the businesses that are closest to their customers are best placed to avoid the threats posed by such changes, and take advantage of any opportunities created by them.

Activity 1.4 Marketing myopia

An article entitled Marketing Myopia by Theodore Levitt was published in the July/August issue of the *Harvard Business Review* in 1960. This article laid the foundations of what "marketing orientation" is (and what it isn't). You should be able to find it through a local library, or failing that, buy a copy online at www.harvardbusinessonline.com (search under "Levitt").

Also, read Hill and O'Sullivan (2004) *Foundation Marketing* (3rd Edition) FT/Prentice Hall, pages 1-26 and the subsequent self-check questions 1-4 and 8-10.

Planning for marketing activity

To ensure that they keep abreast of their customers' changing needs and respond to them in the most effective ways, most "marketing orientated" organisations go through a planning process which helps them determine how best to approach the task of marketing their goods and services. The marketing planning process has three main purposes: to assess the organisation's current position in its market, to set goals for the future, and to determine what sort of marketing activities will enable those goals to be reached. There are five important stages in the planning process.

Marketing audit

This is the process of collecting and analysing information relating to the organisation's **external environment** (the organisation's markets and wider society) and **internal environment** (the organisation's own resources and capabilities). The external audit examines the situation in the organisation's macro- and micro- environment (explained in Session 2), while the internal audit examines the operations of the organisation itself – its efficiency, its profitability, its staff levels, etc.

SWOT analysis

When the marketing audit is complete, the organisation should be in a good position to evaluate its own strengths and weaknesses – to work out what it is good at, and just as important, what it isn't. It will also understand how changes in society and its markets might present opportunities for it to become even more successful, or that create threats that, if ignored, could undermine its effectiveness. These **Strengths, Weaknesses, Opportunities** and **Threats** will indicate what is achievable for the organisation in the future, and can be used to help set realistic and achievable marketing objectives.

Marketing objectives

Drawing up a realistic statement of what the organisation wants to achieve is a vital prerequisite to deciding what types of marketing activities the organisation should be undertaking. In general, these marketing objectives should specify the volume and value of goods and services it intends to sell to its existing customers, and the volume and value of goods and services it intends to sell to its potential new customers. Marketing objectives should be SMART – Specific, Measurable, Achievable, Relevant and Time-related. They are much more than just a wish list for what the organisation hopes to achieve, as they will be part of the rationale and justification for future marketing activities.

Marketing strategies and tactics

The key difference between marketing strategies and marketing tactics is that the former describe the general approach that an organisation will take to the marketing of its goods and services, whereas the latter describe the actual marketing activities that will have to take place to implement the strategies and achieve the marketing objectives. Both strategies and tactics tend to be described in terms of the **marketing mix** – the products, prices, promotional activity and distribution channels that will be used to meet the needs of the customers (plus, in the case of services, the people, processes and physical evidence that need to be in place to deliver those services). But strategies are broad in nature, whereas tactics are specific activities. For example, an organisation's promotional strategy may be to use mass media communications to reach a wide consumer market. Under this strategy, it could use TV advertising, newspaper advertising, or press relations, for example. This would be a tactical decision.

Marketing budget

Marketing activity generates money from sales, but it also costs money. Therefore, an important element of the plan is a budget that predicts how much money will be generated during the period of the plan, and calculates the costs of the marketing tactics that will be implemented to achieve these revenues. Budgeting has a number of purposes for the organisation as a whole, but for the marketing function it is particularly useful as a device that enables managers to monitor how effective their strategies and tactics are. By regularly reviewing actual sales and costs and comparing them with budgeted figures, it is possible to determine how well the organisation's marketing activity is going, and to take corrective action when its achievements do not meet predicted levels.

Activity 1.5 The best laid plans…

IAM publishing is a small business that sells a fortnightly trade magazine direct to insurance brokers across the UK. Annual subscription to the magazine is sold at £60 each. Recruitment advertising space costs around £2,000 per page, and product and service advertising space costs around £1,000 per page. Back issues are sold at £5 each. The Marketing Manager set out an annual marketing budget at the beginning of the year and has just been given the actual figures for the year's trading.

1. Suggest reasons why advertising sales might have fallen so far short of predictions.

2. Why might advertising sales costs be lower than anticipated?

3. Is it worth selling back issues?

4. What type of marketing activity might have helped you to sell a) more recruitment advertising space and b) more product and services advertising space.

5. Propose a plan of action for next year.

IAM Insurance Broker Magazine Annual Predicted/Actual Figures

	predicted annual sales	annual sales budget (£)	actual annual sales	actual annual sales (£)
Advertising sales: recruitment	100 pages	200,000	40 pages	80,000
Advertising sales: products and services	45 pages	45,000	25 pages	25,000
Subscription sales: new subscribers	60	3,600	70	4,200
Subscription sales: renewals	1,240	74,400	1,100	66,000
Sale of back issues	75	375	10	50
Total sales revenues		**£323,375**		**£175,250**
Printing and distribution costs		104,000		110,000
Salaries: advertising sales		35,000		25,000
Salaries: subscription sales		25,000		24,600
Advertising costs		15,000		3,000
Direct marketing costs		8,000		4,000
Exhibitions		5,000		5,000
Miscellaneous expenses		15,000		8,000
Total costs		**£207,000**		**£179,600**
Contribution to overheads		**£116,375**		**-£4,350**

Activity 1.6

CASE STUDY: Levi's

As with all fashion goods, the popularity of jeans goes through peaks and troughs, but evidence suggests that the market for denim is unlikely in the foreseeable future, if ever, to reach the dizzy heights it achieved in the mid 1980s. This was the golden era of jeans, fuelled by the memorable advertising campaign featuring Nick Kamen stripping off down to his boxer shorts in the launderette and waiting for his Levi's – advertising which resulted in a sales boost of 800%! Ever since then the company's advertising campaigns (featuring "flat Eric" and the innovative "Twisted" commercials) have won awards and broken new ground.

But Levi's, as well as other jeans manufacturers, are serving a market that is prey to the whims of fashion, and is facing tough times. Denim sales have fallen massively in the face of competition from other fabrics and styles, such as khakis and cargo pants. Levi's more recent advertising campaigns have failed to excite the consumer in the way that their earlier campaigns did. The rebelliousness of the Levi's brand, much favoured by youth markets and so neatly encapsulated in the '80s ads, is now the hallmark of new brands such as Diesel. 501s, which for so long proved to be a product that met universal needs, have been gradually eschewed by young consumers with a fervent desire to assert their individuality. There's a limit to how many 501s a person will buy, so the Levi's brand, committed for so many years to selling a single look, has found itself in a dead end.

Added to this, the number of young people aged 18-25 in Europe will decline by over five million between 1994 and 2003. Levi's public image has not been helped either by a well publicised legal dispute with Tesco. The company's policy of refusing to allow its jeans to be sold in non-approved retailers backfired when Tesco started selling jeans sourced from outside the EU at knock-down prices. The courts have so far upheld Tesco's view that it should not be prevented from selling Levi's at discounted prices.

Keen to build on the goodwill that still remains in the market for its products, and to move away from its image as 'the brand that your dad wears', Levi's still has its eyes firmly set on the youth market. But the materials will continue to include denim, which despite its decline, Levi's still sees as a core part of its business. The challenge facing Levi's now is to revitalise its range and react positively to a market that favours individuality over conformity, and where unbranded products can have more street-cred than big brand labels.

To do this, the company has segmented its markets into three customer bases: urban opinion-formers; extreme sports; and regular girls and guys; and is creating a range of sub-brands to meet their needs. It has also opened some unbranded retail outlets, called "Cinch!" to target the type of customers it's dubbed "cultural connoisseurs" – fashionable, less mainstream consumers. There is no Levi's branding on the store's fascia, and the store also stocks non-Levi's accessories, including Casio watches, Japanese magazines and art books. There is also a "chill out" room for watching TV.

Questions

1. Try to describe the people who you consider to be in Levi's core market. Then try to define Levi's product. Does your definition include the word "jeans"? Should it?

2. Go to the Levi's web site at www.levi.com to view its current product range. How easy is it to find the right product for you?

3. Would you describe Levi's as a marketing oriented firm? If not, then how would you describe it?

Sources

Day, J. (1999) 'Levi's plans new stores', *Marketing,* 2 September, p7.
Jardin, A. (1999) 'Life for denim in a combat era', *Marketing,* 4 March, p19.
Laferla, A. (1999) 'Surfing the jean pool', *e-volve,* Issue 4, September, pp14-16.
Lee, J. (1999) 'Can Levi's ever be cool again?', *Marketing,* 15 April, pp28-29.
McLuhan, R. (1999) 'Levi's Sta-Prest makes an impression on youth culture', *Marketing,* 25 March, p7.

SUMMARY OF KEY POINTS

- Marketing is the process of satisfying customer needs profitably.
- Relationship marketing focuses on the lifetime value of a customer.
- Societal marketing aims to satisfy the customer and maintain society's well being.
- Marketing is growing in importance.
- Marketing plans are commonly used to determine how best to approach the marketing task.

Glossary of terms

customer orientation: finding out what customers want before deciding what to produce and sell.

economies of scale: when the cost of producing each product falls as the total volume of products being produced increases.

marketing: the management process responsible for identifying, anticipating and satisfying customer requirements profitably.

marketing audit: an evaluation of an organisation's marketing systems and activities.

marketing budget: a breakdown of the expenditure that an organisation sets aside for its marketing activity.

marketing mix: the marketing tools that an organisation can use to influence demand (product, price, promotion and place).

marketing objectives: the goals an organisation is trying to achieve through its marketing activities.

marketing orientation: recognising the importance of placing the needs of customers at the heart of an organisation.

marketing strategies: the marketing principles and direction which the organisation is pursuing.

marketing tactics: the day-to-day implementation of marketing activities.

product orientation: an overriding preoccupation with producing the products a firm would like to make, rather than satisfying customer needs.

production orientation: an overriding preoccupation with sustaining efficient production, rather than satisfying customer needs.

relationship marketing: a concept that emphasises long-term customer value, rather than individual transactions.

sales orientation: an overriding preoccupation with persuading people to buy, rather than satisfying their needs.

societal marketing: an approach to business which considers the interests of society as a whole, as well as trying to satisfy individual customer needs.

SWOT analysis: an evaluation of an organisation's Strengths and Weaknesses, and the Opportunities and Threats facing it.

Self-test multiple-choice questions

1. **Which of the following is most likely to arise when businesses adopt a production orientation?**
   a) Good customer relationships.
   b) Economies of scale.
   c) Environmental change.
   d) Longer supply chains.

2. **A marketing audit examines:**
   a) An organisation's external environment.
   b) An organisation's external and internal environment.
   c) An organisation's accounting practices.
   d) An organisation's social responsibilities.

3. i)   Economic prosperity leads to more complex customer needs.
    ii) Longer supply chains make it easier to understand customer needs.

    Which of these is true?
    a)   **i** only.
    b)   **ii** only.
    c)   both **i** and **ii**.
    d)   neither **i** nor **ii**.

4. **The marketing approach which emphasises the importance of maximising the lifetime value of customers is known as:**
    a)   Sales orientation.
    b)   Relationship marketing.
    c)   Loyalty marketing.
    d)   Societal marketing.

5. i)   **Marketing tactics are the basis on which marketing strategies are designed.**
    ii) **Marketing budgets are used to predict the financial implications of a marketing plan.**

    Which of these is true?
    a)   **i** only.
    b)   **ii** only.
    c)   both **i** and **ii**.
    d)   neither **i** nor **ii**.

Something to think about...

1. Under what circumstances might a marketing orientation not be in the best interests of society?

2. How does sales orientation differ from marketing orientation?

3. Why might you set marketing objectives?

4. For what reasons might a) an accountant or b) a production manager object if a marketing manager suggests launching a new product?

5. What sort of problems might a customer encounter when dealing with a company that has a production orientation?

Session 2

Responding to the micro- and macro-environment

This Session will help you to identify the type of changes that may arise in an organisation's environment, and understand why it is important to respond to these changes. It will examine factors that affect all organisations (the macro-environment), as well as those which are specific to individual firms and industries (the micro-environment).

LEARNING OUTCOMES

At the end of this Session you should be able to:

- List the key external factors that affect an organisation's ability to achieve its objectives.

- Distinguish between factors that arise from the macro-environment and micro-environment.

- Give examples to illustrate ways in which organisations respond to changes in their environments.

- Recognise the dangers of failing to respond to changes in the environment.

STUDY TEXT

An organisation's marketing environment comprises the external events and pressures that have the potential to affect its ability to do business with its customers. These pressures can come from a wide variety of sources – some of them very difficult to predict. A good example is the outbreak of Foot and Mouth disease in the UK in 2001. Farmers may have been well aware of the potentially catastrophic impact that such an eventuality could have on their businesses, but very few in the rural tourism industry would have predicted just what a serious impact the measures to contain the disease would have on them.

Pressures from the external environment can create either opportunities or threats (or both) for the organisation. In order to protect themselves from the potentially negative impact of changes in their environments, and take advantage of any positive changes, marketers need to be constantly aware of the nature and scope of the factors that might affect their fortunes. These factors fall into one of two categories, known as the macro-environment and the micro-environment.

Figure 2.1

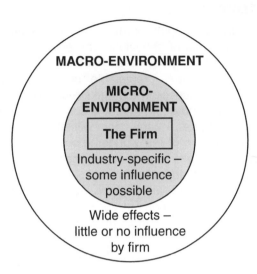

The macro-environment

Forces that are beyond the influence of any one firm or industry are described as being in the macro-environment. Society as a whole is affected by changes in the macro-environment, and there is little, if anything, that any one firm can do to affect these changes. But a marketing-oriented firm will attempt to predict impending changes, so that it can implement marketing activities that will take advantage of them, or at least protect itself from them as far as possible. These changes tend to be one of four types, known as the **STEP factors** (or sometimes PEST factors).

Figure 2.2

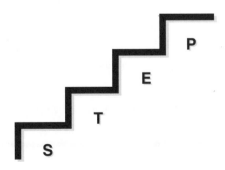

Socio-cultural factors

Changes in the structure or composition of society, or the **culture** that underpins society and determines norms of behaviour, can slowly but surely influence the size and nature of markets for products and services. These changes can take many forms. One of the most predictable changes in society is in the **demographics** of a country, especially the age structure of the population. Simply by monitoring the birth rate and death rate, it is possible to predict the age profile of a country well into the future. A baby boom will lead to a bulge in the teenage population, then an expansion of the workforce, and ultimately a larger pool of retired people, particularly if life expectancy is getting longer. Firms supplying products and services which appeal to specific age groups can anticipate the points at which levels of demand are likely to increase, and set their marketing objectives accordingly. Other changes in society that affect businesses include changing family structure (such as an increase in the number of single-person households and single-parent families; later marriage; and non-family households), wider access to education, and increasing cultural diversity.

Activity 2.1 Statistics.gov

Go to the web site at www.statistics.gov.uk or the statistics section of your library to find out:

- In 2001, what proportion of all live births took place outside marriage? How much has this changed since 1991?

- If a man was alive at the age of 65 in 1971, how many more years could he expect to live? How different is this for a man who reaches 65 in 2001? In 2021?

- How many visits abroad were made by UK residents in 2001? By how much has this increased since 1981?

- What proportion of households had two or more cars in 2000? How much has this increased since 1970?

(The answers to these questions are all in the datasets relating to Social Trends 33 – 2003).

Explain some of the marketing implications of these figures for insurance companies.

Technological factors

New technologies that are specific to a particular industry or market are regularly developed. But some new technologies operate beyond the boundaries of any specific sector, and have the potential to affect everyone's lives. The growth of the Internet as a vehicle for communications is undoubtedly the most significant technological change that the world has seen for many years, and its impact on businesses is already widely felt. Printing and paper industries are threatened as more organisations choose to publish materials on the web instead of on paper. Retailers are threatened as their suppliers choose to deal direct through their own web sites, and new "virtual" retailers set up web sites which perform the same role as they do, but with lower overheads. Small businesses can use their web sites to compete with major corporations, without having to incur the costs of mass media advertising campaigns. Digital TV is set to change the profile of the media, with the rapid increase in the number of TV channels available making it harder to communicate with a mass audience, but easier for advertisers to reach special-interest markets. Biotechnology and genetics are also making major scientific and medical breakthroughs, which may in turn affect agriculture and the food chain, as well as life expectancy.

Activity 2.2 Don't stop the music...

The following table gives details of sales levels of four pre-recorded music formats, LPs, CDs, Audio Cassettes and Singles, in the UK since the early 1970s.

	LPs (m)	Cassettes (m)	CDs (m)	Singles (m)
1973	81.0	9.8	–	54.6
1974	89.5	14.0	–	62.7
1975	91.6	16.5	–	56.9
1976	83.8	16.0	–	56.9
1977	81.7	18.5	–	62.1
1978	86.1	20.6	–	88.8
1979	74.5	23.5	–	89.1
1980	67.4	25.2	–	77.9
1981	64.0	28.7	–	77.4
1982	57.8	31.5	–	78.6
1983	54.3	35.8	0.3	74.0
1984	54.1	45.3	0.8	77.0
1985	52.9	55.4	3.1	73.8
1986	52.3	69.6	8.4	67.4
1987	52.2	74.4	18.2	63.4
1988	50.2	80.9	29.2	60.1
1989	37.9	83.0	41.7	61.1
1990	24.7	75.1	50.9	58.9
1991	12.9	66.8	62.8	56.3
1992	6.7	56.4	70.5	52.9
1993	5.0	55.7	92.9	56.3
1994	4.5	56.0	116.4	63.0
1995	3.6	53.4	139.2	70.7
1996	2.4	46.2	159.7	78.3
1997	2.5	36.6	158.8	87.0
1998	2.2	32.2	175.7	79.4

(Source: British Phonographic Industry)

1. In which year were total sales of pre-recorded music at their highest?

2. By what percentage did the total market for pre-recorded music grow between 1988 and 1998?

3. Between which two consecutive years was the highest percentage increase in CD sales?

4. Plot a graph showing all four formats, to illustrate how the market for pre-recorded music formats has changed over the years.

5. Explain the marketing implications of these figures.

Economic factors

The wealth of a country and its population determines the nature and level of demand for products and services. In affluent Western economies, where the majority of the population has more than enough food to eat, people have disposable income to spend on luxury products. Cars, "designer labels", furniture, and leisure activities will all be major product categories in these countries, and offer good potential for profitable business. But if the economies of these countries move into recession, expenditure on luxuries can fall quickly and substantially, leading to a significant decline in sales revenues for companies in these industries. In less developed countries, much higher proportions of consumer expenditure are allocated to food; but even in these markets, if income distribution is uneven, there may be pockets of wealthy people who will generate sufficient demand for luxury products to make it worthwhile trading there. Other economic changes that may affect an organisation's ability to trade profitably include changes in unemployment levels, taxation policy, interest rates and exchange rates for foreign currencies.

Politico-legal factors

Governments can have a significant influence on businesses, through the policies they implement and the laws they pass. Legislation affecting business tends to fall into three categories.

1. Laws that protect consumers from unscrupulous business practices may affect the implementation of marketing activity in areas such as price-setting, use of customer databases and product safety specifications.

2. Laws that protect firms from each other include copyright and patents, which prevent other firms from stealing your ideas; and import controls, which prevent foreign firms undermining the domestic market by selling goods at unsustainably low prices.

3. Laws are also in place to protect society. They aim to ensure that all members of society are treated fairly and equally, and that the natural environment is preserved. Anti-pollution measures fall into this category, as does legislation like the Disability Discrimination Act, which requires all businesses to facilitate access for disabled people. In some areas, however, self-regulation is in place, rather than a legal framework.

Activity 2.3 Access all areas

It is estimated that there are over 8 million disabled people in the UK, with spending power of around £33 billion a year. Under part II of the UK Disability Discrimination Act, 1995, which came into effect in October 1999, service providers must ensure they do not refuse to serve a disabled customer, offer them a lower standard or manner of service, or less favourable terms than people without disabilities. The Act poses a range of issues for marketers. For example, a consumer may be unable to enter a prize draw because they have impaired sight, or unable to take up a dream holiday because they use a wheelchair. But more commonly, problems arise due to physical access to buildings, such as cinemas, shops and restaurants.

As a group, evaluate the extent to which leisure services, retailers and restaurants in your area have responded to the requirement of the Disability Discrimination Act in terms of providing access for those who are mobility impaired. What sort of threats face organisations who do not provide adequate access?

The micro-environment

Forces over which a firm or industry have some control are described as being in the micro-environment. Events and pressures that occur elsewhere in an industry or a market can, to some extent, be influenced by a firm; depending on the way in which it reacts to them. But in general, as in the macro-environment, a marketing-oriented firm should attempt to predict impending changes and implement marketing activities that will take advantage of them. Such changes might for example stem from new competitors entering the market for the first time; from new distribution channels (like the Internet) becoming available; or simply from sudden increases in demand from the market. Pressures in the micro-environment tend to stem from five sources.

1.   Customers

A **market** comprises people who wish to buy a certain type of product or service. An organisation's customer base may well be drawn from a number of markets. Demand for computers, for example, comes from several different types of market, each of which has special characteristics. Consumer markets buy them for their own use in the home, and levels of demand in that market can be influenced quite significantly by the promotional activities of the computer industry. There are also groups within the consumer market that will experience different growth rates. Home computers are often bought for children to learn or play games on, but adults are also another important group of customers, wanting to use them to manage their domestic finances, or for access to the Internet, or even for running a small business. Organisational markets on the other hand buy computers to enable them to produce and supply their own goods and services, so hardware or software developments that help them save costs through improved efficiency can lead to increases in demand. Reseller markets buy computers to sell to on to others, and demand levels in this market will be influenced by demand from the end-user market. If more and more consumers start buying direct, through the Internet for example, the reseller market will start to decline. By monitoring trends in these different markets, marketers are forewarned of likely increases or decreases in demand, and can adjust their planned marketing activity accordingly in an attempt to influence the market in their own favour.

2. Competitors

In the same way that a business might be serving several different types of market, so it may be facing several different types of competitor. An organisation's competitors may not even be operating in the same industry. For example, a theatre selling tickets for a live performance isn't just competing with other theatres – it is also competing with cinemas, pubs, restaurants and the TV. New competitors can slip into markets almost unnoticed if they come from outside the traditional boundaries of the industry, or compete in a very different way – such as dealing direct through the Internet rather than through established retailers. Changes in the number, type and strength of competitors may require a marketing response. As the number of competitors serving a market grows, so does the likelihood that price discounts will be offered to consumers. New businesses may use special offers to gain a foothold in the market, and this is likely to squeeze the profitability of those already trading. Marketers who track the activities of competitors are best placed to implement tactics that take advantage of gaps in the market where there are no or few competitors, and also to protect themselves from new and aggressive forms of competition.

3. Suppliers

These are important players in the micro-environment, as they control the availability and price of the materials, components and resources needed to create products and services for end-user markets. Changes in supplier practices can have a major impact on an organisation's marketing activities. Late deliveries, faulty goods and unacceptable price levels all create marketing problems. Suppose a publisher is planning a new magazine launch on a certain date, and has booked a major TV advertising campaign to support the launch. That publisher is dependent on a printer to supply the magazines. The printer, in turn, is dependent on a designer to provide the words and pictures to be printed, and paper merchants to deliver the paper on which it will be printed. If any of these suppliers fail to deliver their promised goods and services, the publisher will be generating demand for a new product that isn't available on the newsagent's shelves, and the impact of the launch will be undermined. In monitoring the micro-environment, it is important to identify any changes in the dynamics of supply so that the implications of any impending shortages, price rises, or interruptions in supply can be taken into account in the marketing planning process.

4. Intermediaries

Many organisations use third parties to help them reach their markets as efficiently as possible. These third parties are known as intermediaries, and they can support an organisation's marketing in a number of ways. Some intermediaries take responsibility for an organisation's physical distribution processes, providing warehousing and delivery services. Others take responsibility for marketing services, such as advertising agencies, who create persuasive communications and buy media slots on TV, radio, or the press. But by far the most important intermediaries for most marketers are **resellers,** who provide support by making products and services more easily available to end-users.

Retailers, wholesalers, agents and merchants are all examples of resellers who generate their own revenues by taking a fee, commission or mark-up for distributing other firms' products and services. Marketers are often highly dependent on resellers, who operate at the interface with their end-user customers. Manufacturers of grocery products, for example, are very dependent on large national supermarket chains to ensure that their products are available in the market. Yet these supermarkets are themselves large organisations trying to maximise their own profits. Consequently, important negotiations take place between supermarkets and grocery suppliers about prices, stock levels, and promotional activity – all issues that ultimately affect the customer. Supermarkets may be unwilling to stock a product unless the profit margin on sales is sufficiently high, and are convinced that the manufacturer is doing all it can to promote that product to the ultimate consumer. It is important for marketers to monitor trends in retailing, to ensure that they are selling their products through the most effective intermediaries. With e-commerce, organisations have a choice as to whether to use reseller intermediaries at all, or whether to deal direct with the consumer themselves.

5. Stakeholders

This is a diverse group of organisations and individuals who have an interest in (or can have an impact on) the fortunes of a business. Financial stakeholders, for example, might include banks and shareholders. Banks can determine the rate at which a business can afford to expand, by deciding whether or not to lend any money to implement planned marketing activity. Shareholders too, who will normally require a financial return on their investment in a business, can put pressure on a company to behave in certain ways.

Another important group of stakeholders is the media. Journalists can be very influential over public opinion, and from time to time they take an interest in the marketing activities of businesses. This can take the form of a positive endorsement of activities, or it could result in very negative publicity. National charities, for example, are often criticised in the media for the amount of money they spend on promoting their causes and running their organisations. This can be very damaging to their attempts to raise money, and may be quite unjustified. Some charities see their role as educating the public about the cause they support, not simply generating money for it. If this is the case, it may be quite justifiable to spend large amounts of money on advertising campaigns.

Consumer pressure groups can also influence the effectiveness of marketing activity, and may even determine marketing strategy. Widespread concern over the safety of genetically modified ingredients in food products has led many food manufacturers to abandon any thoughts of increasing profitability by using GM products. Any possible benefits that may arise from the low prices of GM ingredients would be more than outweighed by the bad publicity that surrounds them.

Activity 2.4 Insulting the customer?

The Advertising Standards Authority (www.asa.org.uk) is the self-regulatory body to which members of the public are invited to complain if they consider any advertising (other than broadcast advertising) to be offensive or misleading. The Code of Conduct for advertisers is published on the ASA web site. As society develops, and public sensitivities change, so do the guidelines. But when it comes to taste and decency, there are no hard and fast rules. An advertiser who is deemed to have breached the Code will be asked by the ASA to withdraw an ad, which wastes both time and money, so advertisers will want to do everything they can to prevent a ban. But they still want their advertising to have an impact, and sometimes, the closer they sail to the wind in terms of what is "tasteful", the more effective the message, and the higher the sales that follow. For example, in recent years French Connection has been a regular subject of complaint for its infamous fcuk campaign.

i) On the ASA web site, look at the adjudications dated 4th April 2001, 10th January 2001 and 12th May 1999 to find out what was considered to be acceptable and unacceptable in three of French Connection's ads.

ii) Identify a print or poster ad that you think might contravene the Advertising Code of Conduct, and draft a letter of complaint to the ASA. In your letter, specify the parts or part of the Code that you believe the advertiser may have breached.

Activity 2.5 Webbed feat

Start to compile a directory of useful web sites that a marketer may like to refer to when considering the macro- or micro-environment of an organisation. Include the two sites mentioned earlier in this Session: www.asa.org.uk and www.statistics.gov.uk. You could also include some of the national newspapers and the CIM's own web site www.cim.co.uk.

Also read Hill and O'Sullivan (2004) *Foundation Marketing* (3rd Edition) FT/Prentice Hall, pages 59-84, and self-check questions 3, 6, 9,10.

Activity 2.6

CASE STUDY: Who's online?

The Internet is the fastest growing medium in history. In terms of the time it took to reach 50 million users, radio was the slowest at 38 years; TV somewhat faster, at 13 years; and the World Wide Web has done it in just 4 years. By the end of 2000, 51% of all adults in Britain had accessed the Internet, and 80% of them (a total of over 18 million adults) had done so within the previous month. But Internet usage is not uniform across demographic groups. The proportion of adults who use the Internet decreases with age (see Table 2.1), and the proportion of those aged 16-24 years old continues to show the most dynamic growth of all. Individuals living in households headed by a professional are significantly more likely to have accessed the Internet than those headed by manual workers.

Table 2.1

Characteristic	July 2000	January 2001
	%	%
All adults	45	51
Age groups		
16-24	69	85
25-44	60	66
45-54	49	50
55-64	33	39
64-74	10	15
75+	6	6
Gender		
Male	52	57
Female	39	45
Occupation		
Professional	66	78
Intermediate	58	65
Skilled non-manual	46	53
Skilled manual	31	37
Partly skilled manual	26	33
Unskilled manual	20	27

Source: National Statistics Omnibus Survey – January 2001.
Crown Copyright 2001.

Growth of access in the UK has been meteoric. Although people access the Internet for personal use from a wide range of locations, including the workplace, schools, universities and colleges, Internet cafes, Post Offices and public libraries, by far the most commonplace is the home. In 1998 a mere 9% of households could go online at home using a personal computer, but by the start of 2000 this figure had risen to 25% of households, and by the end of 2000 access from a personal computer at home was possible in 33% of households. Deregulation and technological advances in the telecoms market have kick-started demand for Internet access through WAP phones. By January 2001, 7% of all adults who had ever used the Internet had done so using a phone, compared to less the 1% in

July 2000 and 5% in October 2000. The percentage using Digital TV to access the Internet has remained constant at around 6% since October 2000.

The Internet is used for a wide range of online activities (see Table 2.2).

Table 2.2

Activities	% of Internet users (Jan 2001)
Finding information about goods and services	67
Using email	65
General browsing or surfing	54
Finding information related to education	28
Buying or ordering tickets	30
Personal banking or investment	23
Looking for work	18
Playing or downloading games	20
Using chat rooms or sites	13
Playing or downloading music	15
Using or accessing government/official services	18
Other uses	5

Just as interesting are the reasons given by adults who had never accessed the Internet as to why this was the case. Lack of interest was cited by the highest proportion (41%), particularly those aged 45 and over, followed by lack of access to a computer (28%), the main reason in the 16-44 age group.

Questions

1. List some of the implications of this extraordinary growth of Internet access and usage for marketers targeting the UK consumer. Consider the needs of those producing and selling products that facilitate Internet access, as well as those who wish to use a web site as part of their marketing communications.

2. Who should the suppliers of WAP phones be targeting at the moment? At what stage might they change their emphasis and target a different group? Why might they do this?

3. How might marketers encourage a larger proportion of older people ("silver surfers") to use the Internet for shopping?

Sources

Fortune, 1 February, 1999.

Johnston, A. (1999) 'Welcome to the Wired World', *Research,* November pp22-25.

National Statistics Omnibus Survey – January 2001.

SUMMARY OF KEY POINTS

- Pressures from the external environment can create opportunities or threats (or both).

- The marketing environment comprises a macro- and a micro-environment.

- The macro-environment comprises forces that are beyond the influence of any one firm or industry (Socio-cultural, Technological, Economic and Politico-legal factors).

- The micro-environment comprises forces over which a firm or industry has some control (customers, competitors, suppliers, intermediaries, and stakeholders).

Glossary of terms

competitors: organisations producing products and services that satisfy similar customer needs.

culture: the set of beliefs, values and attitudes that underpin society.

customers: individuals or organisations who buy a firm's goods and services.

demographics: the patterns and trends of population and social structures.

industry: a group of organisations producing similar goods or services.

intermediaries: organisations who help goods and services to be transferred from producer to consumer.

macro-environment: events which influence more than one industry and over which firms have **very little** control.

micro-environment: forces which directly affect the running of a business and over which that business has **some** control.

market: a group of people who wish to buy a certain type of product or service.

resellers: organisations which take a fee, commission or mark-up for making other firms' products and services more readily available to end-users.

stakeholders: organisations or individuals who have an interest in or influence over the fortunes of a business.

STEP factors: the Socio-cultural, Technological, Economic and Politico-legal factors in an organisation's macro-environment.

suppliers: organisations who provide the resources needed by other firms to produce their own goods and services.

Self-test multiple-choice questions

1. **Which two of the following lead to changes in a country's demographic profile?**
    a) An increase in average life expectancy.
    b) A decline in the tendency to marry.
    c) A change in attitudes towards the environment.
    d) An increase in average disposable income.

2. **i)   Customers in a reseller market buy products and services to satisfy their own needs.**
    ii) Resellers are examples of marketing intermediaries.

    Which of these is true?
    a) **i** only.
    b) **ii** only.
    c) both **i** and **ii**.
    d) neither **i** nor **ii**.

3.   Which one of the following arises in an organisation's micro-environment?
   a)   Changes in economic policy.
   b)   The development of a new technology.
   c)   Increased immigration.
   d)   Shortages of raw materials.

4.   i)   **As the number of competitors serving a market increases, so does the likelihood that price discounts will be offered to customers.**
   ii) **The competitors in a market may come from more than one industry.**

   Which of these is true?
   a)   **i** only.
   b)   **ii** only.
   c)   both **i** and **ii.**
   d)   neither **i** nor **ii.**

5.   Over which of the following is an organisation likely to have least influence?
   a)   Articles published about it in the newspapers.
   b)   The service levels of its retailers.
   c)   Its prices.
   d)   Consumer legislation.

Something to think about...

1.   In what ways might a bus company be affected by government transport policy?

2.   If interest rates in a country are low, to what extent might this influence the demand for mortgages provided by banks and other financial institutions?

3.   How do you rate the Internet as a shopping experience? Are there things you would buy online that you would not buy in the High Street and vice versa?

4.   If your company sells package holidays, who are your competitors?

5.   To what extent are universities and colleges vulnerable to changes in the demographic profile of the population? How might they respond to these changes?

Session 3

Gathering secondary data

This Session will help you to understand why marketing information is of great value to organisations, and give a range of suggestions as to where you should start looking for the type of information that will help you understand your customers and your marketing environment. It also explains how you can extract a wealth of valuable information through the Internet.

LEARNING OUTCOMES

At the end of this Session you should be able to:

- Recognise the situations in which marketing information can be helpful.

- Distinguish between primary and secondary data.

- Identify a range of sources of secondary data.

- Use the Internet to find a range of useful information for solving marketing problems.

STUDY TEXT

Needless to say, a lot of marketing decisions are taken every day without anyone gathering any information at all. So what's wrong with acting on a hunch, or basing decisions on anecdotal evidence of what's going on in your market? The main reason for taking the trouble to gather information, about customers or competitors, is to improve the likelihood that you will make sound marketing decisions. Only when you are in possession of information that helps you really understand the nature of your market and your industry will you be able to evaluate the marketing options open to you and decide upon the most effective course of action.

It is vital to be able to answer questions such as 'who are my customers?', and just as importantly, 'who are my potential customers?', before decisions are made about the types of products or services to produce and sell, or the prices to charge. A flow of information into an organisation enables it to identify and define marketing opportunities and threats more rapidly, diagnose marketing problems more accurately, and generate more effective marketing plans.

What type of information do we need?

Marketers need two types of information to help them make good marketing decisions.

Firstly, information should be gathered from the **external environment,** particularly information about customers and competitors, to shed light on the nature of markets and industries. It is especially important to identify any trends and changes that might affect the potential of a business to generate profitable business. For example, knowing about trends in unemployment or income distribution might give an organisation a forewarning that their markets will experience growth or go into decline. Knowing that a rival firm has just launched a new product using more reliable technology will flag up a potential threat, as customers may defect to the competition. Assessing how confident consumers feel about spending money rather than saving it (the "feel-good factor") can help firms in markets for non-essential goods and services to calculate likely demand for things such as holidays, home-improvements and new cars.

But businesses also need information from the **internal environment** of their own organisations to help them understand the extent to which their marketing strategies and tactics are achieving their objectives. Information is required to help managers understand how effective their pricing policies are for example. It can also reveal what proportions of products are sold through which retailers, and whether TV advertising produces more enquiries per £ than press advertising. It can indicate when a product is no longer generating viable levels of revenue, or should be discontinued in favour of a new product.

Having decided what information is required, the marketer is then faced with the task of either **finding** that information (if it is already available, having been collected for another purpose or another organisation) or **generating** it (using appropriate research techniques to collect the facts and figures). Information that already exists in some form is known as **secondary data**, and the process of finding what you need is known as **desk research**. Information that has to be generated for a specific marketing purpose is known as **primary data**, which is gathered from market research activity (see Session 4).

Secondary data

Secondary data is extremely valuable to marketers. Because it already exists, the costs of searching for it are normally much lower than the costs of generating information yourself. Also, some information that exists would be impossible to collect from scratch, as it is based on historical evidence that is long gone.

Statistics that describe population trends are a good example of this. It would be both physically almost impossible and prohibitively expensive for any individual firm to collect information about a country's births, marriages and deaths. In order to know what the population trends are, the firm would have to monitor events continuously over a very long period of time. Consequently, the task of generating useful information like this tends to be left to governments, who then make it available to businesses and the public.

Although secondary data is valuable, it does have its limitations. The precise type of information you need may not be available, either because no one has ever collected it, or because the owner of the information refuses to release it to you (or wants to charge you a lot of money for it!). You may also have doubts about the accuracy of the information. The Internet is an invaluable means of distributing information worldwide, but there is no authority monitoring whether the information supplied by web site owners is accurate, up to date or truthful.

Activity 3.1 Soft furnishings

Your team has been asked by a client to assess the market potential for a new product concept – a piece of software that will enable users to try out possible interior design solutions for their homes.

- List the information that you think might be useful.

- List the sources of secondary data where you might find some of this information you would like.

- Allocate each member of the group a source to investigate.

- Pool your findings and prepare a group presentation to your client.

Internal data

Information that is owned by the organisation itself is described as internal data. This is particularly useful to marketers as it relates specifically to the organisation itself, and can potentially offer valuable insights into the nature and behaviour of an organisation's own customers. It may, however, be held in different departments throughout the organisation. So whilst in theory it is available to inform marketing decisions, in practice it might be difficult to get hold of in a form that can be easily used.

There are many sources of internal information that might interest marketers, but the following are the most widely used.

The customer database

When customers' names and addresses are recorded by organisations and linked with details of their purchasing behaviour, the information collected is known as a customer database (whether or not these records are held on a computer). This database can be an invaluable tool for investigating customer characteristics and behaviour. For example, an Internet or mail order retailer will be in a position to profile its customer base in terms of its geographic spread (nationally and internationally), its expenditure levels, its product preferences, and its frequency of purchase. This investigation can be used to group together buyers with similar characteristics and purchasing patterns (known as market segments, as explained in Session 6). Then, when it is clear what types of people are most likely to be among its customers, the retailer is in a position to design promotional campaigns, special pricing offers, service levels and new product ranges that are most likely to appeal to these types of people, and target their marketing activity accordingly.

Customer databases are also very useful for monitoring trends and identifying the root of marketing problems. A supermarket chain experiencing a decline in sales might be losing business because a competitor's supermarket has just opened in the area. It would be possible to deduce whether or not this is the case by examining the database and seeing whether the decline in sales has arisen from those postcode areas nearest the new store.

Accounting records

A company's accounting department keeps very precise details of both sales and costs. Records are kept of who has bought how many of what types of products at what prices, so it is usually quite easy for accountants to identify sales trends and work out the profitability of different product lines. This type of information enables marketers to see when a product is coming to the end of its life cycle (see Session 7), and will help determine how much of the marketing budget should be allocated to different products and services.

Activity 3.2 Profit profiles

A firm selling three products has announced the following (simplified) profit statement.

	£
Sales	2,300
Less all expenses	1,600
Profit	**700**

However, when the Marketing Manager made further investigations, she found the following profit breakdown by product.

	Product analysis		
	A	B	C
Sales	900	600	800
Less all expenses	400	900	300
Profit	**500**	**-300**	**500**

1. Why might this information be of interest to marketers?

2. Under what circumstances might you choose to discontinue product B? Why might you continue to market this apparently loss-making product?

3. Which product is performing better, A or C?

Customer feedback

Suggestion boxes, records of complaints and feedback forms on web sites are all valuable sources of information about what customers do and don't like about your products and services. Although this type of information is generally gathered to respond to the service issues that arise when dealing with customers, it also provides marketers with clues as to how best they can improve the value they offer to customers. It may even point to viable gaps in the market where demand exists but nobody is serving the market.

Web site monitoring reports

Information about who visits which parts of your web site is invaluable in the planning and evaluation of your marketing activity. A simple count of the number of site visits and specific page visits made each day tells you how large an audience you are reaching and enables you to see which of your web pages are attracting the most interest. How people find your web site is also of interest. Do they come through search engines? If so your web site strategy may be working well. Do they tend to arrive at your web site from a specific web address? This indicates that other forms of advertising, or even word of mouth, are generating interest in your business.

External data

Information that is generated and owned by other organisations, rather than by the organisation itself, is known as external data. Useful external data may come from a wide range of sources, many of which are available for consultation completely free of charge through public libraries and the Internet. Other data may be owned by private organisations who may well charge for it.

Among the most common sources of external data used by marketers are:

Government statistics

Governments around the world collect data and publish statistics that they use to help them identify social and economic trends, for the purpose of managing the economy and maintaining social welfare. These statistics can also be very useful to marketers. In the UK, a summary document called the Annual Abstract of Statistics contains a comprehensive set of government statistics, including figures describing the UK economy, industry, society and demography. This is all presented in easy-to-read tables with useful explanatory notes and definitions. It is just one of a very wide range of reports based on surveys carried out for government departments, all of which can be accessed through the web site at www.statistics.gov.uk

Trade Associations and Professional Bodies

There are few industries in the UK that are not represented in some way by a trade association. It is common for these organisations to collect data from amongst their membership, and generate information relating specifically to trends in their particular industry. Professional bodies, such as the Chartered Institute of Marketing, Chambers of Commerce and the Institute of Purchasing and Supply, represent interests across industries, and can often supply more general information relating to economic, social or technological developments affecting business.

The Trade Press

A very wide range of newspapers, magazines and journals are published in English and other languages, providing a constant supply of news and information to industry and business. These range from the very general, such as the Financial Times and Management Today, to the very specific, aimed at a very small but highly targeted readership. Many are available on the Internet as well as in print.

Syndicated research

Specialist research reports are published by commercial market research agencies, focusing on specific market sectors, countries or topics. Sometimes this type of information is available only to subscribers. Sometimes it is available for a one-off purchase. Euromonitor, for example, regularly publishes reports on markets as diverse as alcohol and soft drinks, catering and telecommunications. Another well-known syndicated service is The Target Group Index, a survey based on 25,000 interviews a year, which takes place across the UK, generating continually updated information on the usage of over 4,000 brands in 500 product areas by consumers aged 15 and over. The data is widely accessed by organisations serving consumer markets to help them understand more about the behaviour of their target markets. For example, the survey data can be used to identify the TV programmes watched and newspapers read by people who are the heaviest drinkers of fruit juices. Information which can then be used to maximise the impact of advertising expenditure.

Activity 3.3 Site inspection

Compare and contrast the following web sites:

- www.abc.org.uk

- www.bpaww.com

- www.apa.co.uk

- www.ppa.co.uk

What are these sites? Who might be interested in using the data they provide? Which is the most user-friendly web site?

Searching for information using the Internet

Until recently, most sources of external secondary data were available only from libraries or for sale from private sources. But the rapid development of online databases means that vast amounts of information can now be accessed from **web sites** through the **Internet**, dramatically improving the speed and convenience of obtaining secondary data. This can be particularly quick if you know the web site address you need. All you have to do is type the **Uniform Resource Locator** (URL) into your web **browser**, and you will reach the site you are looking for. Some web sites may be password protected if they contain information that is only available to paying subscribers, but you can nearly always get through to the organisation's **home page**, where you can find out more details of the services being offered and how to subscribe.

If your search is for a company or organisation, but you do not know the actual address of the site, you could start by having a quick guess at its likely URL. Most begin with www. and end with a suffix which indicates the organisation type. UK company web sites are likely to end with .com or .co.uk; not-for-profit organisations are likely to be .org or .org.uk; and academic institutions are likely to be .ac.uk. So if you wanted to look at the web site for Kodak, you might type www.kodak.com into your web browser, which does indeed take you through to the Kodak web site. Similarly, www.birmingham.ac.uk takes you to the web site of the University of Birmingham, and www.oxfam.org.uk takes you to this charity's web site. However, such guesswork is not infallible. You might think that www.rsc.org would get you to the Royal Shakespeare Company's web site, but in fact you will end up at the Royal Society of Chemistry!

Activity 3.4 Be a better Internetter!

Go to the web site at www.netskills.ac.uk to access the free online introductory "Tonic" course that will help you use the Internet more effectively. Look through the course to find a tutorial that will help you make better use of search engines. There are also tutorials showing the kinds and range of data available on the Internet for students.

Also, read Hill and O'Sullivan (2004) *Foundation Marketing* (3rd Edition) FT/Prentice Hall, pages 124-131 and the subsequent self-check questions 1, 6 and 9.

Using a search engine

If you don't have a web site address, but simply want to surf the net to find information that will help you investigate a particular marketing problem or issue, then finding what you want is not quite so straightforward. There is no logical index of content to the **World Wide Web**, so you will have to use a search engine to look for the material you want. Basically, a search engine is a web site that logs the words from millions of documents on the web. When you type in the keywords associated with the topic, organisation or theme you want to investigate, the search engine will list all the web sites it can find that contain that word or words. When you select the ones you want, it will connect you to them. However, because the search engines log the content of many millions of web sites, each keyword you type in can return thousands of results! This can leave you with the overwhelming task of deciding which ones are most likely to be of use to you. Needle and haystack spring to mind?

Successful searching

There are three important keys to finding marketing information on the Internet. Firstly, select a search engine that you find easy to work with. Although search engines differ in appearance and function, in most cases there are more similarities than differences, and the basic search principles remain valid across all search engines. For example, Ask Jeeves (www.askjeeves.co.uk) is a comprehensive and user-friendly search engine; and an online interactive tutorial is available at www.learnthenet.com to help you use search engines more effectively.

Secondly, it's important to specify the most relevant keywords associated with the topic you are investigating. It is often quite simple to find a company or organisation: just type in the organisation's name. But more complex concepts need a little more thought. For example, to find out the scale on which shoe sizes are sold in the US, put the words "shoe size" into a search engine and see how long it takes you to get what you want. It is possible to use the search engine more effectively if you use some simple techniques that narrow down the results and bring the most relevant web pages to the top of your results list. One such technique is to connect all your search terms with the word "and". When you do this the search engine will only retrieve the web pages that contain all the keywords. So if you type in "US and shoe and size" you might find that the first web site your search engine finds for you is the very useful 'US, UK and European Clothing and Shoe Size Equivalents'.

Finally, remember that whilst the Internet is a valuable route to obtaining secondary data for marketing purposes, the information it can provide is neither monitored nor evaluated. "Unofficial" web sites claiming to represent consumer views of products and services can provide an interesting insight into customers' opinions of your products, but remember, they may not be particularly representative of the total customer base.

Activity 3.5 Engine manual

Write a set of instructions to someone who hasn't used the Internet before, to help them use a search engine of your choice, to find useful secondary data about the market for dishwashers.

Activity 3.6

CASE STUDY: Grocery Mosaic

A company called Experian sells a useful form of secondary data aimed at marketers who are interested in understanding more about consumer grocery-buying behaviour. Known as "Grocery MOSAIC" it is a classification system that predicts the grocery buying habits of each of the UK's 1.65 million postcodes, each of which comprises around 15 households.

To compile the system Experian combined a wide range of statistical information from extensive surveys and government statistics to classify all UK grocery buyers into one of ten distinct types. The residents of every postcode in the country have been labelled as being a particular "type", depending on a range of factors, including where they are most likely to shop, how price conscious are they, what type of newspapers do they read, the frequency with which they shop, etc.

For example, one of the grocery buying "types" has been dubbed the "Speciality Singles". Comprising 8.2% of all grocery shoppers in the UK, people of this type tend to live in Greater London and other densely populated urban areas, where there are plenty of easily accessible grocery outlets. Usually single, these shoppers are likely to enjoy speciality and luxury products, often of a cosmopolitan nature, for themselves or their friends, and partners with whom they may be sharing a flat. They insist on convenience, are unlikely to be loyal to any one store, and make several trips a week to retailers near their home. Many do not have cars because of the availability of public transport, and they tend to read broadsheet newspapers, particularly The Guardian, The Independent and the Financial Times. They are frequent cinema-goers, like new technology and Internet shopping, telephone banking and home delivery services.

Organisations who buy access to Grocery MOSAIC do so for a range of purposes. They may compare their own customer databases with the MOSAIC types to try to understand what sort of people buy from them. They may use the system to help them identify the most appropriate site to locate a new retail store; or target a door-drop promotion to appropriate neighbourhoods.

Questions

1. Do you think you are typical of the sort of people who live in your street? If so, describe the grocery-buying patterns that you think you share with your neighbours. If not, why not?

2.   What might be the advantages and disadvantages of using profiling systems based on secondary data, such as Grocery MOSAIC, to implement a door-drop campaign to target consumers?

3.   List any other ways in which you can envisage Grocery MOSAIC being used.

Sources

Grocery MOSAIC fact sheet, Experian, 2001.
www.business-strategies.co.uk

SUMMARY OF KEY POINTS

- Secondary data exists before a research exercise begins, having been collected for another purpose or another organisation.

- Internal data is owned by the organisation and relates to the activities of that organisation. It includes customer databases, accounting records, customer feedback and web site monitoring reports.

- External data is generated externally and may come from a wide range of sources, such as government statistics, trade associations, the trade press and syndicated research.

- A wide range of secondary data can now be accessed through the Internet, dramatically improving the speed and convenience of obtaining secondary data.

Glossary of terms

browser: a piece of software which allows you to view the Internet on your computer. Common browsers include Netscape Navigator and Microsoft Internet Explorer.

desk research: the collection of secondary data.

home page: the main web page for a person or organisation. Usually leads to other pages that then have a link back to it so you don't get lost on the web site.

Internet: the world's largest computer system, which links together thousands of computer networks internationally.

primary data: facts and figures that are collected specifically to provide the information that will help achieve the research objectives.

search engine: a program that helps users to find information on the web by entering a word or combination of words.

secondary data: facts and figures that are already available, having been collected for another purpose or another organisation.

syndicated research: market research data which is generated by a market research firm and sold to many organisations.

Uniform Resource Locator (URL): the address system for the world wide web, which leads to each web site's unique address.

web site: any collection of linked web pages published by an organisation (or an individual) on the Internet.

world wide web: information held on the Internet as a series of linked documents which can be accessed through web browsers.

Self-test multiple-choice questions

1. **Desk research is the process used to generate:**
   a) Primary data.
   b) Government statistics.
   c) Secondary data.
   d) Syndicated research.

2. **Which two of the following are not sources of internal data?**
   a) Customer databases.
   b) Accounting records.
   c) Professional bodies.
   d) Competitors' web sites.

3. i)   **A search engine can be used to help you surf on the Internet.**
    ii) **A web browser is a piece of software that allows you to view the Internet on your computer.**

    Which of these is true?
    a)   i only.
    b)   ii only.
    c)   both **i** and **ii**.
    d)   neither **i** nor **ii**.

4. **Which one of the following is not a mechanism for gathering customer feedback?**
    a)   An in-store suggestion box.
    b)   A telephone complaints line.
    c)   A feedback form on a web site.
    d)   A Uniform Resource Locator.

5. **For which two of the following reasons might a marketer be interested in an organisation's accounts?**
    a)   To enable them to monitor their sales budgets.
    b)   To enable them to monitor the organisation's share price.
    c)   To assess the profitability of different product lines.
    d)   To enable them to generate primary data.

Something to think about...

1. What type of information does the government generate that might be useful to marketers?

2. What are the key limitations of secondary data?

3. A magazine publisher holds a lot of secondary data in the form of a database of subscribers. In what ways might the publisher use that information for marketing purposes?

4. Is it possible to collect too much secondary data?

5. What sort of records might an organisation's accounts department keep that could provide useful secondary data for the marketing department?

Session 4

Research techniques

This Session will help you to identify the most appropriate techniques to use when generating marketing information. It explains the key differences between qualitative techniques to investigate how people think, feel and behave, and quantitative techniques that investigate the extent to which people think, feel or behave in similar ways to others.

LEARNING OUTCOMES
At the end of this Session you should be able to:

■ Distinguish between qualitative and quantitative research methods.

■ Distinguish between continuous and ad hoc research.

■ Understand the concepts of a population and a sample.

■ Prepare a questionnaire and explain a range of data collection methods.

■ Explain how focus groups and depth interviews should be conducted.

■ Discuss the advantages and disadvantages of email and web-based research.

■ Identify situations in which experimentation or observation might be appropriate.

STUDY TEXT
There are many questions that simply cannot be answered by referring to information already in the public domain, or that exists elsewhere in your organisation. If this is the case, then you are faced with the task of collecting primary data to help you generate the information you need.

Collecting primary data
You may need information to answer a specific question relating to a particular marketing situation you face. Why have sales declined by 30% this year? Which colours and styles do customers find most attractive in our new product range? What images does our brand name conjure up in people's minds? To answer

these questions, you will need to conduct a programme of **ad hoc research** – one-off investigations to study specific issues. Ad hoc research can be very helpful at the time, but may not have any long-term value. **Continuous research** however, is designed to be of long-term value. This is the process of regularly collecting information from the market over an extended period of time, so that trends can be identified and predictions made on the basis of the trends observed.

Primary research, whether continuous or ad hoc, will fall into one of two categories, depending on whether you want to know about **how** people think, feel or behave, or **how many** people think or behave in certain ways.

Quantitative research

Quantitative research is the term used to describe research techniques that answer the "how many" question. The most common technique used is a survey.

Surveys

Surveys use questionnaires to generate quantitative data, enabling useful generalisations to be made about people's behaviour, attitudes and opinions. In marketing, surveys are generally used to help understand and predict the behaviour of customers and potential customers, to gather information about the products and services they use, what they use them for, when they use them, and how often they use them. They can also reveal opinions about products and services (which may or may not be based on the experience of having used them!).

The survey process is a cost-effective method for finding out information about large numbers of people, as it relies on collecting the views of a small sample of people who are likely to represent the views of the population as a whole. Statistical analysis is then applied to the answers given to enable conclusions to be drawn as to how likely it is that the views they express are held by others.

The quality of information generated by a survey is heavily dependent on the design of the sample of people selected to respond, the questionnaire itself, and the way in which the questionnaire is delivered or administered to respondents.

Sampling

The choice of people to respond to survey questions involves a number of decisions. Firstly, the researcher must decide upon the type of people who are relevant to the survey (the population of interest), and identify them in some way (create a sampling frame). Then decisions have to be made as to whether to ask questions of all the relevant people (conduct a census) or just some of them (select a sample).

Population of interest: The purpose of sampling in quantitative research is to select people to answer questions whose responses will be representative of the population as a whole. Therefore it is essential to define the entire group of people from whom a researcher would like to obtain information. For example, if an insurance company wants to assess the quality of its customer service, it could do this by collecting the views of those who have asked for a quotation from the organisation in the past five years. Alternatively, it could ask just those who have taken out policies, or even just those who have claimed on their policies. There are no hard and fast rules as to how a population of interest should be defined. A judgement has to be made as to who is appropriate, depending on what the survey is trying to find out.

Sampling frame: The list of people belonging to a population of interest is known as a sampling frame. Sometimes it is very easy to compile a sampling frame. For example, an insurance company will have a computerised database that gives names, addresses and phone numbers of all enquirers, policy-holders and claimants. When a complete sampling frame such as this exists, it is possible to conduct postal, telephone or email surveys with the chosen respondents. However, in other circumstances, such a list neither exists nor can be compiled, so a data collection method has to be chosen that gives access to the whole of the population of interest. To investigate the market for swimwear, it would probably be best to interview people on the street outside a public swimming pool or near a beach, as there is no such thing as a national list of "swimmers".

Census: The size and availability of an accurate sampling frame will determine whether it is more appropriate to conduct a census of all members of the population of interest, or to select only a sample. It should be relatively easy to gather views from all the members of a CIM study group, because the group will be relatively small and the sampling frame is complete (the names of all the individuals in the class are known). The advantage of a census is that its findings reflect the views of the entire population of interest.

Sample selection: Whenever it is impossible to contact everyone in the population of interest, decisions have to be made as to how to go about selecting a small proportion of the population to respond to the questionnaire.

Simple random sampling (rather like drawing numbers out of a hat) is sometimes used, giving every person in the population of interest an equal chance of being selected to respond to a questionnaire. However, this process can be impossible if there is no complete sampling frame, as well as logistically difficult and expensive to administer. Consequently, researchers often take a more pragmatic view and use techniques known as non-probability sampling, which enable them to select respondents who are relatively easy to reach. Often, in an attempt to replicate the random sampling process as far as possible, they will look for categories of respondents that reflect the relative size of these groups in the population of interest. This is known as quota sampling. For example, if a population of interest is defined as all adults who have attended an orchestral concert in the past 12 months, the quota sample might include two gender groups and three age groups:

- 45% male, 55% female.

- 15% aged under 25, 40% aged 25-60, 45% aged over 60.

Sample size: Having decided on an appropriate sampling method, decisions have to be made as to how many people should be selected to respond to the survey. This is a complex issue. Financial, managerial and statistical factors all have to be considered. Larger samples cost more money, but can provide greater accuracy in reflecting the views of the whole population of interest.

Non-statistical approaches to determining overall sample size are usually adequate, and rules of thumb are used based on past experience of similar surveys. 500 is often considered to be an adequate sample size for market research surveys, but political pollsters tend to interview 2,000 people when assessing the voting intentions of the UK electorate.

Activity 4.1 New cars by region

In some parts of Great Britain people are more likely to drive new cars than others. In the period 1996-98, the percentages of people in each region driving cars of different ages were as follows:

	Age of Car		
	Under 3 years	3-6 years	7 years or more
Great Britain	26	30	44
North East	24	34	42
North West	31	30	39
Yorkshire and Humberside	27	29	44
East Midlands	25	30	45
West Midlands	26	31	43
East Anglia	25	29	45
London	23	28	49
South East	26	30	44
South West	19	27	54
England	25	30	45
Wales	25	31	44
Scotland	33	30	37

Source: Regional Trends, 1996-1998.

Use spreadsheet software such as Microsoft Excel to create bar charts and pie charts to illustrate these figures. Compare the two formats and comment on which is better at depicting the differences between the regions.

Data collection

A range of approaches can be taken to the process of gathering the required information, each of which has its own unique advantages and disadvantages.

Interview surveys involving face-to-face communication between interviewer and respondent can be particularly useful when large populations are of interest and suitable respondents can be found in limited geographical areas. Interviewers can help people to complete the whole questionnaire in the right order, clarifying questions that are not understood, encouraging full answers to open-ended questions, and presenting visual materials relating to questions. The cost of face-to-face interviewing however can be high, and questions must be kept simple, as respondents have to understand them aurally and are required to give immediate responses.

Telephone surveys are a popular alternative to the face-to-face interview. This method preserves many of the benefits from interpersonal contact discussed earlier, without incurring such heavy costs. It benefits from the convenience of being able to contact a wide geographical spread of respondents from a central location, which minimises the need to travel, thus saving time and money. However, the effectiveness of the telephone can be undermined by the sample being limited to those with phones, as well as resistance to all forms of telephone marketing due to the intrusive telesales techniques used by some businesses. Furthermore, selected respondents may refuse to participate (it's easier for people to say "no" over the phone) or terminate the conversation before completing the questionnaire.

Mail and email surveys. Administering questionnaires by post is popular, as a mail survey can reach widely spread populations of interest, and incurs neither interviewer wages nor telephone bills. Questionnaires can be relatively long, as respondents can fill them in at times convenient to them, and can cover sensitive issues which may be answered honestly if a promise of anonymity is given. Alternatively, email can be used to reach populations of interest that are likely to comprise of individuals with Internet access – business respondents and students are the most common. This incurs still lower costs than using postal services, but limits the sample to those who have email and are active users. Sadly, the response rates to both mail and email surveys can be very low, and no interviewer assistance can be given, so incomplete returns are common, particularly if the questionnaire is long.

Self-completion and web site surveys are usually the least expensive method of all. Self-completion questionnaires are often made available to groups of people at specific events or in certain situations, such as those travelling on a train, sitting in a theatre or visiting a tourist attraction. However, more and more questionnaires are now being designed for web sites, enabling interested parties worldwide to respond. But as the respondents decide for themselves whether to pick up the questionnaire and answer the questions, the sample is likely to comprise a disproportionate number of people who have strong feelings about the topic of the survey. Those with more moderate views are less likely to be represented. If the questionnaire is placed on the Internet a second bias is introduced, as respondents will, by definition, be technologically more competent than the average person.

Questionnaire design

The style, length, layout and wording of questionnaires influences the willingness of respondents to give their opinions, as well as the quality of information generated. Shorter questionnaires tend to elicit more considered responses than longer ones, but there are no hard and fast rules as to how many questions should be asked. For a short questionnaire only include questions which provide data relating to the objectives of the survey. The wording of individual questions is equally important. **Closed questions** are preferable to **open-ended questions**, as they are easier to analyse in a consistent way. Each question should be evaluated against a series of criteria. Questions should be:

- **Short** – questions longer than 20 words can be difficult for respondents to grasp quickly, particularly when answering face to face or over the phone.

- **Specific** – if two issues are introduced in the same question the respondent may have different views on the two issues, but will be prevented from separating them if a single overall response is requested.

- **Impartial** – leading questions, in which words or phrases carry overtones that influence respondents to respond in a particular way, should be avoided at all costs.

- **Clear** – avoid using long words, ambiguous statements and complex terminology, as respondents who do not understand a question will either miss it out altogether or, worse still, guess at its meaning and give a response to the question they think is being asked.

- **Inoffensive** – questions about sensitive issues such as salary, age, social class and ethnicity should be carefully worded and placed at the end of the questionnaire.

Before a questionnaire is administered it should be tested on a few people typical of the people being included in the sample. This is known as the pilot stage, which helps ensure that the questionnaire is adequate for collecting the information you want.

Activity 4.2 Driving forward

The Government White Paper, 'A Strategy for Sustainable Development for the United Kingdom', aimed to encourage a safe, efficient transport system, that would provide choice, minimise environmental harm and reduce congestion. New technologies and cleaner cars would be part of the solution, but new approaches to travel, living and working would also be needed. With this in mind, the attitudes of people in the UK towards measures that could be taken to discourage car use were investigated in 1998, as part of the British Social Attitudes Survey by the National Centre for Social Research. The findings were as follows:

	Might use car even more (%)	Might use car a little less (%)	Might use car quite a bit less (%)	Might give up using car (%)	Makes no difference (%)
Gradually doubling the cost of petrol over the next ten years	1	31	23	5	38
Greatly improving the reliability of local public transport	–	28	27	6	37
Greatly improving long distance rail and coach services	–	25	22	4	47
Charging all motorists around £2 each time they enter or drive through a city or town centre at peak times	0	23	21	7	45
Cutting in half long distance and coach fares	0	23	24	7	43
Making parking penalties and restrictions much more severe	–	20	18	4	54
Charging £1 for every 50 miles motorists travel on motorways	–	18	15	6	58
Special cycle lanes on roads around here	–	10	11	3	73

1. Which do you think would be the most effective ways of discouraging car use?

2. The measures shown above in **bold** have the potential to generate revenues from motorists. What other information would you need to know before you are in a position to calculate which of them might generate the most money?

Qualitative research

The reasons why people behave in a particular way, or hold certain opinions, are not usually best explored using a survey. A survey is a mechanistic process that deliberately attempts to limit the range of responses people give to the questions being asked, and therefore it is not very sensitive to revealing the reasons behind observed behaviour and attitudes. So to answer questions about **how** people think, feel or behave you may need to conduct some qualitative research, using interviews that are designed to probe beneath the surface of the responses. These normally take one of two forms:

Depth interviews are prolonged one-to-one interviews, during which the interviewer asks questions on a series of topics. S/he is free to phrase the questions as seems most appropriate and return to the most interesting points raised by respondents and probe them further. The interviewer will have little more than a checklist of issues to explore and will encourage full and explanatory responses from interviewees.

Focus groups (also known as group discussions) involve an interviewer, known as a moderator, who chairs a discussion between a group of six to eight respondents. The moderator has a minimal role in the discussion and simply intervenes to keep the conversation on the right lines, preventing it from wandering away from relevant topics, and acting as a catalyst for new ideas when a subject is exhausted. The moderator must also ensure that even shy participants are encouraged to express their views. Focus groups are often observed through one-way mirrors so that the non-verbal communication of the group can also be monitored.

A successful focus group has three major advantages over depth interviews. Firstly, it is quicker and cheaper than interviewing respondents individually. Secondly, groups can provide a social background that reflects the fact that many decisions made by an individual are taken in a group context and are influenced by others. Depth interviews do not provide the restraining influence of others' opinions. Finally, the range of opinions being expressed in a group discussion can stimulate people to articulate their own beliefs, attitudes, opinions and feelings. There is no such stimulus in depth interviews.

Activity 4.3 Designing a depth interview

In 1998, the BBC axed its regular children's slot on the speech radio station Radio 4, because not enough children were tuning in. But a few years later, the broadcaster is tentatively returning to children's programming. The justification for this was not that children's attitudes to speech radio have changed, but that the BBC sees its duty, as a public service broadcaster, to try and encourage a habit of listening to speech. Programmers believe that radio is a more active medium than television, as it helps develop the listening skills that are critical to early development.

The Controller of Radio 4, Helen Boaden, recognises that the majority of people who listen to the new programme, "Go4It", will be adults, but says 'if only ten percent are children, that's ten per cent more than we had before.' She and the programme's producer, Olivia Seligman, have decided on a magazine format for the programme, with the very first show featuring a top pop group, Olympic rower Steve Redgrave, and author Philip Pullman reading a serialisation of his novel *Clockwork*. The new show is aimed at 8-10 year olds, and marks a radical departure from the format that previously filled the children's slot – high-quality Sunday teatime dramas.

As a group, devise two depth-interview frameworks – one to be used with parents, one with their children (aged 8-10), to help you understand their attitudes towards speech radio. Each person in your group should then interview one family. If possible, encourage the family you are interviewing to listen to "Go4It" before the interview, so that they can also give you their views about the programme. Before you conduct your research, you should read the section of the Code of Conduct of the Market Research Society that refers to interviewing children, to ensure that you are using appropriate procedures for your interviews (www.mrs.org.uk).

Source: Dodd, C. (2001) 'Are you listening children?' *Radio Times,* 14-20 April, p 42.

Activity 4.4 A qualitative proposal

Statistics from the Office of the Rail Regulator report the causes of complaint by passengers about rail services. Recently over half the complaints reported were about poor train service performance. Passenger train operators received 1.1 million complaints, equivalent to 122 per 100,000 passenger journeys, and an increase of 8% over the previous year. However, this increase should be viewed in the context of a rise of 5% in the number of journeys in the same year.

Complaint by %	%
Train service performance	55
Train and station quality	13
Fares and enquiries	12
Information at stations/on trains	5
Complaint handling	2
Other	13

Source: Office of the Rail Regulator

Write a proposal for a piece of qualitative research to investigate ways in which rail services could be improved.

Observation and experimentation

Two further research techniques may be useful in certain circumstances.

Observation involves watching people, their behaviour and their actions, or observing the results of those actions. It is a useful data collection method when human actions and reactions can be viewed, monitored, and recorded, and there is no requirement for the understanding of motivations, feelings or attitudes. Observation can be quantitative, in that the numbers of people acting in similar ways are noted, or qualitative, by recording in detail the ways in which a more limited number of individuals respond. It is a technique that is commonly used by market research agencies. For example, they might study TV viewing habits by attaching monitors to TV sets in households to record when a TV is switched on and off.

Experimentation is a technique borrowed from the sciences. Researchers set up experiments by initiating a limited trial of one element of marketing activity and then monitor the results. Provided all the factors are kept constant, except the one being tested, any divergence from the norm can be attributed to the activity being tested. If a supermarket wishes to test customer price sensitivity to its own-brand products, it may, for a limited period of time, raise the prices of certain lines by 10% while keeping others constant. Changes in sales levels during the period of the trial can be used as an indicator of customer price sensitivity. Experiments tend to be quantitative in nature, as they attempt to generalise about relationships between elements (known as variables) and enable predictions to be made.

Activity 4.5 Researching research

In this Session you have been given an outline of a range of research techniques that can be useful for generating marketing information. Many books have been published on the subject, which give much more detail of these techniques, and how they should be implemented. Compile a database (using Microsoft Excel, Access etc.) containing a bibliography of titles that could help you in the future when you want to implement a programme of research.

You will need to think of how to categorise the books you find. You might like to group them according to whether they are general books, or whether they specialise in either quantitative or qualitative research. You may like to indicate which libraries near you stock these titles. Be sure to note the full title, author(s), date of publication, name of publisher and ISBN reference, in case you need to order the title from a bookshop or through the Internet.

To start your search, try:

- Your own library's catalogue.

- The web sites of The Chartered Institute of Marketing and the Market Research Society.

- The online bookseller at www.amazon.com.

Also, read Hill and O'Sullivan (2004) *Foundation Marketing* (3rd Edition) FT/Prentice Hall, pages 131-148 and self-check questions 5, 7, 8 and 10.

Activity 4.6

CASE STUDY – Marks & Spencer (M&S)

M&S, arguably the most powerful High Street brand in the UK, grew from a market stall in Leeds at the end of the 19th Century to become a global retailer at the start of the 21st Century. Yet in March 2001 the company closed its direct marketing operation and international outlets to concentrate on its core business of serving UK consumers. M&S's shoppers had gradually been drifting away, allured by more trendy high-street offerings.

The blip in M&S's fortunes was widely attributed to the failure of the company to anticipate the changing shopping habits of its core middle-class English customer base. Prior to the turn of the century, M&S had been suspicious, if not hostile towards the idea of conducting customer research. The company culture valued shop-floor experience over market research techniques to tell them what their customers wanted.

Famously, former Chairman and Chief Executive Sir Richard Greenbury was reported in the *Daily Telegraph* as saying he saw "no need" for the customer satisfaction studies conducted in the mid 1990s. Had he taken them more seriously he might have seen the writing on the wall about the gradual defection of his customers towards upmarket boutiques and large discount stores.

Faced with a sales crisis in 2000, the company's new management created a new division known as a "customer insight unit", charged with the task of getting M&S back in touch with its customers. The organisation's marketing research department, which employed just three researchers in 1998, grew to 20 staff. Each of the company's business units – beauty, lingerie, home, women's wear, men's wear and children's wear – is now represented by a dedicated researcher, with senior research managers to pull their findings together, and link them with other sources of data, such as database information from the 4.5 million M&S store card users.

Marketing research for a clothing company holds particular challenges. No matter how good your research it is practically impossible to predict demand for fashion items, where tastes change continually and stock has to be ordered up to 12 months before garments reach the shops. To wait for the research findings could mean missing the boat altogether. As a result, researchers have to be aware of long-term trends, as well as looking at the whole experience of shopping for the M&S customer – from store layout and design, to the assortment of merchandise offered in each outlet. The results of the new emphasis on research have been encouraging. Luc Vandervelde, the chain's new Chief Executive, announced a turn-round in financial results in 2002, telling the press 'Last season brought the first signs of recovery. Today's figures confirm it: the customers are coming back to us. We are gaining their hearts and their wallets, but it is still the beginning. There's plenty of room for further improvement'.

Questions

1. If you were the Director in charge of planning next year's children's wear collection, list the information you would like the customer insight unit to provide to help you decide what to stock.

2. Suppose you wanted to run a series of focus groups to help you understand perceptions of M&S's men's wear. How many groups would you like to run, and what sort of people would you invite to each group?

3. Do you agree that research cannot predict demand for fashion items? If not, then what type of research might generate useful information?

Sources

Savage, M. (2001) 'Full Marks?', *Research*, March, pp22-23.
Finch, J. and Treanor, J. (2000) 'Big may still be beautiful for M&S', *The Guardian*, 8th November.
Rankine, K. (2002) 'Marks and Spencer's recovery gathers pace', *Daily Telegraph* (Money Section), 11th April.

SUMMARY OF KEY POINTS

- Primary data provides information to answer specific questions relating to a marketing situation.

- Quantitative research reveals how many people think or behave in certain ways.

- Surveys use questionnaires to generate quantitative data.

- Qualitative research reveals the reasons why people behave in a certain way or hold certain opinions.

Glossary of terms

ad hoc research: an investigation to provide information about a specific issue.

closed question: a question which provides a limited number of possible answers for the respondent to choose between.

continuous research: an investigation which is repeated on an intermittent basis over a period of time.

depth interview: a prolonged one-to-one interview in which the interviewer probes the answers given by respondents.

experimentation: an investigation to measure the relationship between marketing variables.

focus group: a group interview conducted by a moderator.

observation: a research technique based on watching people's actions and behaviour.

open-ended question: a question which allows respondents to reply in their own words.

population: the total group of people from whom information would be useful.

qualitative research: an investigation to generate information about how people feel and why they behave as they do.

quantitative research: an investigation to discover how many people hold similar views or display particular characteristics.

questionnaire: a standardised set of questions designed to gather data which relates to the research objectives.

quota sampling: selecting questionnaire respondents to reflect certain characteristics of the population of interest.

random sampling: giving every person in the population of interest an equal chance of being selected to respond to a questionnaire.

sample: a small proportion of the population which is representative of the views of all its members.

sampling frame: the list of people who comprise a population of interest.

survey: a data collection method which makes a systematic record of the responses of a number of people to the same questions.

Self-test multiple-choice questions

1. i)   **Ad hoc research is conducted over a period of time to enable marketers to identify market trends.**
    ii) **Ad hoc research can involve the collection of either qualitative or quantitative data.**

    Which of these is true?
    a)   **i** only.
    b)   **ii** only.
    c)   both **i** and **ii.**
    d)   neither **i** nor **ii.**

2. **Which one of the following is not true about a focus group?**
    a)   A focus group is useful for investigating why people behave in a particular way or hold certain opinions.
    b)   A focus group is an example of a qualitative research technique.
    c)   Sensitive or personal issues are best explored in a focus group than in a depth interview.
    d)   A moderator is used to ensure that participants' conversations keep to the topic under investigation.

3. **Which two of the following are true of web site surveys?**
    a)   Marketers have little control over the sampling as respondents decide for themselves whether to go to a web site and whether to answer the questions.
    b)   On a web site open-ended questions are preferable to closed questions, as it is easier to analyse the responses in a consistent way.
    c)   Web site surveys can reach a wider sample of customers than a face-to-face survey.
    d)   Web site surveys are the most appropriate mechanism for conducting a census.

4. **Which research technique uses questionnaires to generate quantitative data?**
    a) Depth interview.
    b) Observation.
    c) Experimentation.
    d) Survey.

5. **The population of interest is...**
    a) The population of a country.
    b) The entire group of people from whom a researcher would like to obtain information.
    c) An organisation's customer base.
    d) A random sample of the population of a country.

Something to think about...

1. What might be the disadvantages of a cinema using email research to find out about customer satisfaction?

2. If you wanted to investigate men's attitudes towards the use of foot deodorants, which research method would you use?

3. Under what circumstances might you consider conducting a self-completion survey?

4. How reliable are the findings from surveys published in magazines?

5. What difficulties might you experience if you wanted to run a focus group amongst 16-18 year olds to find out about their attitudes to sport?

Session 5

Consumer behaviour – how do people buy?

This Session will help you understand why people buy certain types of products and services, and what affects their decisions as to which products and services to buy. It explains how people go about their purchasing decisions, and how to distinguish between those who are buying for themselves and their families, and those who are buying on behalf of organisations.

LEARNING OUTCOMES

At the end of this Session you should be able to:

- Distinguish between consumers and industrial buyers.

- Identify a range of factors that can influence buyers' decision making.

- Recognise the different people who can affect a purchase decision.

- Understand the different processes people go through as they make their buying decisions.

- Explain how the process of buying will vary for different types of product.

STUDY TEXT

Because marketing is the business function that attempts to build mutually beneficial relationships between organisations and their customers and potential customers, some understanding of the nature and behaviour of customers is vital, as it should underpin the design of marketing strategies and tactics.

Consumers and organisational buyers

It is important to make a clear distinction between customers, on the basis of what purpose they have in buying products and services. They fall neatly into two groups. **Consumers** buy goods and services for their own use, for their families or their households. The entire population of a country are potential consumers, in that everyone needs to acquire the products they need to live, and therefore will make purchases that satisfy their own personal needs. **Organisational buyers** on the other hand, make purchases on behalf of their organisations – not for their own use. Retailers, for example, buy a wide range of finished goods from manufacturers and wholesalers, with the purpose of making a profit by reselling them to consumers. Manufacturers buy a wide range of components and raw materials, with the purpose of making a profit by creating their own products to sell to retailers, wholesalers or consumers.

The implications of this distinction between consumers and organisational buyers are significant. Different factors influence the types of products and services they prefer to buy; different people are involved in the decisions about what to buy; and the process by which they go about making a purchase can be quite different too. These differences are picked up again in Session 12, which looks more closely at organisational marketing.

Activity 5.1 Terrific tariffs

Mobile phone companies offer a range of tariffs to their phone users, which in theory makes it possible for consumers to choose the deal that matches best the ways they use a mobile phone at the lowest cost. Different tariffs are available to suit people who want to pay each time they make a call, or those who want to take out an annual service contract. It is even possible to select between schemes that offer cheaper deals in the evenings and weekends, special deals for those who send a lot of text messages, and a business scheme offering good rates for heavy daytime users.

Scheme	Line rental (£ per month)	Talktime included per month	Standard call charges (£ per minute)			Other services (£ per minute)		
			Peak	Off Peak	Weekend	Answer-phone	Text messages	WAP calls
A	17.99	100	.10	.05	.05	.10	.12	.10
B	14.99	1000 off peak	.40	.02	.02	.40	.12	.10
C	17.50	75	.10	.02	.02	free	.05	.10
D	25.00	150	.15	.05	.05	.09	.06	.05
E	40.99	800	.18	.05	.02	.05	.12	.10
F	14.99	25 text messages	.25	.02	.02	.25	.12	.10
G	75.00	unlimited	free	free	free	free	.05	.10

Identify the characteristics of the consumers who might be attracted by each of these deals. How easy is it for them to make the selection that suits them best? In the light of your analysis, do you have any advice for mobile phone companies?

Influences on the decision-making process

Consumers' buying decisions are influenced strongly by their psychological characteristics, their social environment and their personal circumstances. Marketers have very little control over these factors, but must take them into account when planning their marketing activities.

Figure 5.1

Influences on consumer behaviour

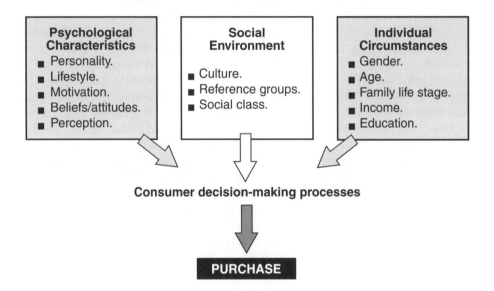

Consumers' **psychological characteristics,** such as their personalities, the things that motivate them, the lifestyles they choose to lead, the beliefs they hold and the attitudes that are attached to those beliefs, can all make a big difference to their views about the types of products and services that would meet their needs best. The value of branding (see Session 7) is closely tied in with this. Whilst people's physical needs for a product such as a pair of sunglasses may be very similar, their individual psychology may influence the type of sunglasses they buy. Those whose physical appearance is very important to them, and who believe that what they wear reflects the sort of person they are, may well be prepared to pay more to acquire a pair with a designer label. They probably value style over functionality. But anyone who holds the attitude that the role of sunglasses is to protect their eyes from the sun, and that designer labels are a marketer's way of making more profits, is much more likely to buy an unbranded pair from a chain store.

A consumer's **social environment** will also affect choice. For example, factors such as our culture – the prevailing beliefs, values and behaviours that underpin our society – influence the types of products that we value. The tremendous growth in the number of women in the workplace over the past 30 years has created huge demand for labour-saving domestic products, such as washing machines and dishwashers. The decline in religious observance has contributed to the demand for retailers to open on Sundays. Reference groups also influence our purchasing. These are the professional, social and family groups with which we interact. Of these, our families are often the most influential group. If our parents have always bought a particular brand of baked beans, banked with a certain bank, been keen theatre-goers, or selected a certain brand of car, then the chances are we will be predisposed to behave in the same way. But children also influence the choices made. They are receptive to advertising messages, but may not have any purchasing power, so their influence tends to be exerted through cajoling and persuasion! A **social class** is another group to which we belong, but in a different way. Membership of a social class is subconscious. It is, however, demonstrated by a combination of facts, including the beliefs we hold, our occupations and what we own. It is also reflected in the products and services we choose to buy. For example, the "professional" classes may be more likely to attend opera, eat mayonnaise and read the *Financial Times,* whereas the "working" classes are perhaps more likely to attend bingo, eat salad cream and read the *Mirror!*

Consumer behaviour

Activity 5.2 Class act

Each person in your group should prepare a short paragraph about themselves that will give some clues as to their social class. Read out your statement to the rest of the group and discuss which social class you believe you belong to. Now consider the following range of products and discuss to what extent you believe your buying behaviour for each of them is related to your social class.

- Newspapers.
- Toothpaste.
- Supermarkets.

Draw conclusions as to the extent to which social class is a good predictor of buyer behaviour and the usefulness of the social classification.

Which class are you in?

Marketers tend to use the ABC scheme to determine a person's social class, which is based on the occupation of the head of the household.

Figure 5.2

Group	Social status	Occupation of head of household
A	Upper middle	Higher managerial, administrative or professional.
B	Middle	Intermediate managerial, administrative or professional.
C1	Lower middle	Supervisory or clerical, junior managerial, administrative or professional.
C2	Skilled working	Skilled manual workers.
D	Working	Semi-skilled and unskilled manual workers.
E	Unwaged	State pensioners or widows, casual or lowest grade workers.

77

Consumers' **individual circumstances** affect their purchases, sometimes in very obvious ways. Men are more likely to wear aftershave than women! Young single people are more likely to go to clubs than parents with young children. Those on higher incomes are more likely to go on long-haul holidays than those on low incomes. The **family life cycle** is a useful model for thinking about how needs for products and services are likely to change during a person's life, and the marketing implications of this. For example, those who are newly-wed with no children are likely to have considerable disposable income to spend on their houses and leisure time. But the arrival of children diverts much of this income to cover childcare costs, food, clothing and activities for them.

Figure 5.3

Wells & Gubar (1966) Family Life Cycle

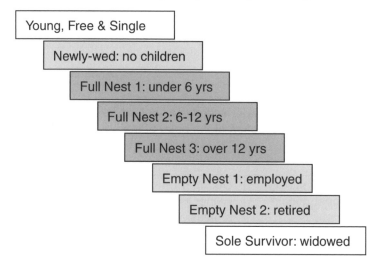

To illustrate the combined impact of these influences, consider an 18-year old male who lives in a rural area and is thinking about buying his first car. The dominant psychological influence on his decision to buy a car is likely to be his need for independence, particularly as in the UK you increasingly need personal rather than public transport – rural bus services being very limited. But his ultimate decision as to which model to buy will also be influenced by a whole host of other factors, including his income, his attitudes towards comfort and speed, his beliefs about the reliability of different brands, the extent to which his parents will support his choice, the cost of insurance for his age group, whether he wants the car to go to work or simply for pleasure, and the image he wants to put across to his friends.

Activity 5.3 Just the ticket

Suppose you wanted to arrange a surprise treat for your brother and his family to celebrate his 40th birthday. You have decided that you will either buy tickets for an opera (his favourite music) at the Royal Opera House or for a match at Aston Villa Football Club (his favourite team). You want to buy tickets for two adults, one of whom is a wheelchair user, and two children, aged 10 and 14. You would like to do this using a credit card transaction online. To what extent do these web sites help you complete your transaction with ease? If you gave up trying, why was this? All else being equal, which organisation are you most likely to buy from?

The decision-making unit

A lot of buying decisions are made under the influence of not just one, but a whole group of people, collectively known as the **Decision-Making Unit (DMU),** who will assume different **buying roles** for different purchases.

The **initiator** is the person who first conceives the idea of making a certain type of purchase, such as a child wanting sweets, a student needing a floppy disk, or an employee who has booked time off work and wants to go on holiday. **Influencers** are the people who give advice that then informs the buying decision. They usually have some experience of buying the type of product being considered, so different people tend to influence different buying decisions. Colleagues might offer you advice to help you choose a new computer, but may not have any suggestions on buying a burglar alarm or taking a holiday in Thailand. The **decider** will evaluate all the information available and assess the best fit between their needs and the alternative products and services that can satisfy those needs. Factors such as product features, availability, price and image, will all be weighed up by the decider, who will determine what is bought. The **buyer** is the person who actually performs the transaction, exchanging money for goods. The buyer may also be the decider, but not necessarily. Parents often buy items that their children have selected, and married couples may only have one nominated credit card signatory who makes all their purchases. Finally, the **user** is the person for whose benefit the purchase is being made. In the case of a gift, the user will have had very little,

79

if anything, to do with the rest of the decision-making unit. But in the case of a person who buys a sandwich for lunch, all of the roles are likely to be taken by the user themselves!

The decision-making process

Figure 5.4

Consumer decision-making process

Many of us have agonised over purchasing decisions. Should I buy the more expensive version that comes with a full guarantee? Where can I find out which product has the best reputation for reliability? Does the green one suit me better than the blue one? What happens if I don't like it when I get home? All of these questions and more are part of the decision-making process – the series of thought processes we go through as we make our buying decisions. The process is recognised as having five key steps. It is important for marketers to understand these, to enable them to identify the most effective tactics for influencing consumer choice throughout the decision-making process.

Problem recognition (Perception of Need)

At the very start of the decision-making process is the consumer's recognition that something is missing – that life could be better if a product or service were bought! This recognition can spring spontaneously from consumers themselves, for example, if they run out of toothpaste, or if their neighbours buy a new car. However, it can also be triggered by persuasive marketing communications, such as tempting advertising imagery, authoritative comment in the press, or cut-price deals, so a great deal of promotional activity is designed to prompt consumers into thinking of buying something.

Information search

Having identified what they might like to buy, consumers look for information to help them choose the best brand or model. For purchases that are very routine, such as grocery products, toiletries and soft drinks, consumers do not look far. They simply search their own memories. Provided a brand was satisfactory last time they bought it, they are very likely to buy the same brand again. On the other hand, when they are facing a new type of buying decision for a relatively expensive product or service, such as a holiday or a car, they are likely to search extensively for information in magazines or from the Internet, and ask friends for their opinions. The key task for marketers at this stage in the decision-making process is therefore to ensure that accurate information is as widely available as possible.

Evaluation of alternatives

The information search enables consumers to draw up a shortlist of products or brands. So the next stage for them is to identify the relative merits of the different options on that list. The criteria on which this evaluation takes place will depend on the nature of the product and the nature of the consumer. Price is often an important factor. Some services, like car insurance, for example, are thought of as commodities, and many customers will choose the insurer who offers them the lowest premiums. Other products, however, are far less price sensitive, and consumers are willing to pay more for brands which they believe offer a better performance, or are more reliable or stylish. It is very important for marketers to understand the main criteria on which the evaluation of alternatives is made, so that they do not fall into the trap of reducing their prices unnecessarily, believing it to be the only way to get to the top of consumers' shortlists.

Purchase

Even when they have selected their chosen products and brands, consumers can still be diverted from actually making a purchase if the transaction is not straightforward. You may find a product you like on a web site, and attempt to place an order, but if the web site doesn't permit online credit card transactions, or if the supplier is unable to deliver it at a convenient time, you may give up and use a High Street retailer instead. The elements of marketing activity that are particularly influential at this stage in the decision-making process are related to the distribution process, through which products and services are made available to consumers. Breakdowns in customer service at this stage can ruin an intended purchase.

Post-purchase evaluation

The way we feel about the products we've bought depends on the extent to which our expectations have been met. If the product's performance matches or surpasses our expectations we will be satisfied or even delighted. But when it falls short we are dissatisfied, and the larger the gap between expectations and performance the greater the dissatisfaction. A key lesson for marketers to learn therefore is not to over-claim the benefits of their products, as dissatisfied customers will not be repeat customers, and worse still, they may tell many others of their disappointment.

Activity 5.4 Many happy returns?

Prepare a set of guidelines for sales staff at a retail store of your choice, to help them deal with customers who return products they claim to be faulty and ask for a refund. In your guidelines you need to consider:

- Should there be different guidelines for people who return goods after 6 months?

- What about returns where the product looks as if it has been heavily used?

- What if the customer sees a fault that is simply a design feature?

- What are the consequences of a customer going away dissatisfied?

Purchase classes

The speed at which consumers linger over each stage of the decision-making process will depend to a large extent on the importance of a purchase to them, and the extent to which they are familiar with making this type of purchase. Five distinct categories of behaviour can be observed, creating five product purchase classes.

Impulse purchases occur when consumers buy products that they didn't really intend to. The perception of need for these products is very low, so marketers have to make attempts to stimulate a need. Wide availability, strong brand awareness and high-profile promotional campaigns can all trigger impulse purchases. It is no coincidence that supermarkets sell well-known confectionery brands next to the checkouts!

Consumers spend a little more time on the decision-making process for **routine purchases** such as coffee, soap and pasta, but they don't bother with an extensive information search or evaluation of alternatives, as they buy this type of product on a regular basis and know what they like. Marketers can give themselves a pat on the back if their strategies and tactics generate a large base of loyal customers for whom their product or service becomes a routine purchase.

Familiar purchases are similar to routine purchases, in that they are known types of product; but consumers may be willing to spend some time on a limited information search and evaluation of alternatives. Suppose a manufacturer of tinned soup, which has a loyal and long-standing customer base, changes its original recipe. This may alienate some customers, who may then begin the process of replacing that brand on their shopping lists. Promotional campaigns for competitive products might tempt people to re-consider their normal brands. If a supermarket own brand is offering "two for the price of one", or their usual brand is out of stock at their normal retailer, then some consumers may be persuaded to abandon the brand.

From time to time we all face **unfamiliar purchases.** These arise when we buy a type of product for the first time. Because we are uncertain of what to expect from the product, we may go through quite an extensive information search and lengthy evaluation of alternatives. Insurance is a good example. The first time we take out a policy, we may search widely for the best deal. But having done that, the renewal may become a routine purchase, unless our post-purchase evaluation suggests we could have done better with another company.

Finally, there are some products and services that are **critical purchases** for us, as the consequences of making a bad decision could be serious, or even catastrophic! Critical purchases tend to be for expensive products that we buy only occasionally. There is a high risk (often financial) to getting it wrong. Houses, cars and pension policies are good examples of these. Marketing them is very dependent on the provision of high-quality information, and a respected brand name, both of which help consumers overcome their lack of confidence with the product.

Activity 5.5 Guard your card

Online transactions are becoming more and more popular with Internet users, though fears still exist about the security of transactions. Use the Internet to investigate how online credit card transactions can be set up. (Either start with a search engine, or try the service provider at www.worldpay.com).

Also, read Hill and O'Sullivan (2004) *Foundation Marketing* (3rd Edition) FT/Prentice Hall, pages 89-106, and self-check questions 3, 4, 8, and 9.

Activity 5.6

CASE STUDY – Sunny Delight

Sunny Delight, having been launched in April 1998, reached a position as the UK's number 3 soft drinks brand by August 1999, and was applauded as being the only consumer product of the decade to take less than a year to make it into the league table of top brands. Annual sales topped £160 million, not far off the £190 million generated by established soft drinks manufacturer Pepsi.

The success of the brand was predicated on a number of key marketing activities. First and foremost were the successful efforts to position Sunny Delight as a healthy drink that children would enjoy. Launched in the US by Procter & Gamble, Sunny Delight had been available there since 1964, where it was sold on ordinary shelves alongside squashes and carbonated drinks. The UK launch, however, saw blanket distribution of Sunny Delight through supermarkets, but in chiller cabinets, next to the fresh fruit juices, giving the impression that it was made from superior ingredients than other soft drinks. The launch was backed by a £9 million advertising campaign with the slogan 'The great stuff kids go for'. And indeed they did. It proved to be as popular with children, for its taste, as with their parents, for its supposedly "healthier" qualities.

However, the success of the brand attracted media attention, and soon newspapers and consumer programmes started to attack Procter & Gamble for misleading the public. Despite its appearance and its in-store locations, those who examined the label carefully found that Sunny Delight was concocted from a cocktail of ingredients which included no mention of orange juice, but high proportions of sugar and water with vegetable oil, thickeners, vitamins and colourings, and just 5% citrus juice! The publicity around the brand was not helped by a report in a medical journal describing "Sunny Delight syndrome". A five-year-old girl who commonly drank 1.5 litres of it each day turned yellow from an overdose of betacarotene, the additive used to give the drink its orange colour. The message 'Like all soft drinks, Sunny Delight should be consumed in moderation' now appears on each bottle.

Questions

1.   What types of psychological characteristics do you think might typify a "Sunny Delight" buyer? What influences in the social environment might have led parents to buy Sunny Delight for their children?

2.   Into which "purchase class" do soft drinks like Sunny Delight fall? How might media coverage such as Sunny Delight attracted affect the purchase class of a product?

3.   If you were the Marketing Director for Sunny Delight, what approach would you now take to restore consumer confidence in the brand?

Sources

Doward, J. (1999) 'Harnessing Pester Power', *The Observer*, 15 August.
Lawrence, F. (2001) 'The Last Straw', *The Guardian*, 11 April.
Teather, D. (1999) 'Unreal thing takes on the real thing', *The Guardian*, 11 August.

SUMMARY OF KEY POINTS

- Consumers buy goods and services for their own use, or for their families and households.

- Organisational buyers make purchases on behalf of their organisations.

- Consumers' buying decisions are influenced strongly by their psychological characteristics, their social environment and their personal circumstances.

- The group of people who collectively influence a buying decision are known as the decision-making unit.

- Products can be classified into purchase classes according to the level of effort people are prepared to put into buying them.

Glossary of terms

buying role: the nature of input a person has into the decision to buy a product or service.

consumers: individuals who buy products and services for themselves or on behalf of their households.

decision-making process: series of steps a buyer takes in selecting a product or service from a series of alternatives.

decision-making unit (DMU): a group of people who exert an influence over a decision to buy a product or service.

family life cycle: the stages of formation and progression of a typical family.

organisational (or industrial) buyers: those who buy products and services on behalf of the organisations they work for.

purchase class: a classification which indicates the level of effort a buyer will exert in deciding what to buy.

social class: a group of people with similar levels of wealth and power who share similar values and attitudes.

Self-test multiple-choice questions

1. i) **A retailer is an example of an organisational buyer.**
   ii) **Consumers buy goods and services for their own use, or for their families or households.**

   Which of these is true?
   a) **i** only.
   b) **ii** only.
   c) both **i** and **ii**.
   d) neither **i** nor **ii**.

2. **Which two of the following are true?**
    a) Consumers making an impulse purchase will seek information to help them make a decision.
    b) Consumers making a routine purchase will seek more information than consumers making an unfamiliar purchase.
    c) Consumers making a critical purchase seek information to help them minimise the risks of buying the wrong thing.
    d) An unfamiliar purchase can ultimately become a routine purchase.

3. **Which of the following is not a member of the consumer decision-making unit?**
    a) Buyer.
    b) Decider.
    c) Retailer.
    d) User.

4. **i) A social class is a group to which a consumer subconsciously belongs.**
    ii) Social class "B" comprises skilled manual workers.

    Which of these is true?
    a) i only.
    b) ii only.
    c) both i and ii.
    d) neither i nor ii.

5. **The purchase of which of the following products is least likely to be influenced by a person's family life stage?**
    a) Car.
    b) Perfume.
    c) Breakfast cereal.
    d) Holiday.

Something to think about...

1. Who are the members of the decision-making unit when you go on holiday? When you go to the cinema? When you go to the hairdresser?

2. For which purchase classes do you spend the longest time evaluating alternative products or services?

3. Which do you think has more influence on the brand of toothpaste you purchase: Your social environment? Your age and gender? Or your personality and lifestyle?

4. In what ways does your decision-making process change when you are buying something as a gift rather than for your own consumption?

5. Which information sources do you consult when deciding which insurance company to use for travel/household/car insurance?

Session 6

Target marketing – how do we find customers?

This Session will help you recognise the circumstances under which mass marketing, differentiated marketing and target marketing strategies are likely to be effective. It will illustrate a range of bases on which markets can be segmented and explain the main criteria for effective market segmentation.

LEARNING OUTCOMES

At the end of this Session you should be able to:

- Distinguish between the different approaches to marketing.

- Understand the concept of market segmentation and how it is used.

- Recognise the different bases on which consumer markets are segmented.

- Explain why not all bases for segmentation are appropriate for all products and all markets.

STUDY TEXT

When an organisation has acquired a good understanding of its customers and potential customers, and has evaluated its own capabilities, it is in a position to consider how to approach its markets. There are four generic ways in which an organisation can do this.

Approaching the market

Figure 6.1

Undifferentiated marketing

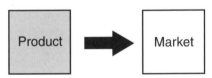

Organisations that attempt to build a customer base using a **mass marketing** approach take the view that their potential customers are fairly similar to each other, so the most efficient way of marketing to them is to design a single product or service concept, and use a single set of marketing strategies and tactics to attract them. This has proved to be a very successful approach for organisations like McDonald's and Coca-Cola, both of which have brand images and narrow product ranges that are recognisable the world over. By using an undifferentiated approach, which treats the whole world as a single mass market, organisations can reap tremendous benefits from economies of scale. Because they take a uniform approach their costs are kept low. This in turn enables them to keep their prices down to appeal to the widest possible market, yet still remain profitable. However, it is not appropriate for every organisation. As shown in Session 5, many markets comprise consumers whose needs, although physically very similar, are psychologically very different, so a "one size fits all" approach is often rejected. Industrial markets for raw materials and components, such as computer memory chips and machine tools, are probably the best suited to a mass marketing approach, as these types of product are designed to meet very specific technical needs, which do not vary in the same way that human nature does.

Figure 6.2

Differentiated marketing

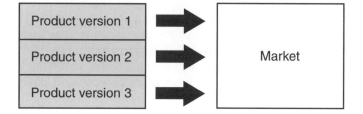

In many markets variety is important. This is particularly the case in industries like food and drink, where customers need a range of alternatives to keep them interested. In these circumstances a **differentiated marketing** approach may be more appropriate than mass marketing. Even Coca-Cola, famous for its monolithic global approach, sells a range of slightly different products – different packaging, different sugar levels and different sizes of bottle. Indeed, a differentiated marketing approach, whereby organisations produce ranges of variant products aimed at the same broad market, can be very effective at maximising sales. Marketers seek to extend their product variety to plug any gaps in distribution and prevent competitors gaining a foothold.

Figure 6.3

Target marketing

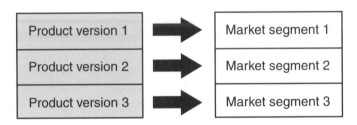

A differentiated marketing approach, although recognising that people have different needs that cannot be satisfied by a single product, still presents them with a uniform set of marketing strategies. Essentially, although the market is being offered variety, it is still addressed as a single entity. A **target marketing** approach takes a step beyond this, recognising that groups of people with similar needs often have physical, behavioural and psychological characteristics that set them apart from the population as a whole. Developing specific marketing tactics aimed at such groups (known as segments), rather than tactics designed to appeal to everyone who might be interested in a particular product, can be both effective and cost-effective. This makes it possible to identify the segments that are most likely to be interested in a particular product or service, and design marketing campaigns specifically to meet their needs.

Car manufacturers, for example, aim to attract families with their "People Carriers", executives with their luxury saloons, young men with their sports cars, businesses with their vans and short-distance town and city drivers with their compact models. This is an example of a **multi-segment marketing** strategy, in which an organisation uses target marketing to approach a number of different segments in the market – here covering practically all the available customers. An even more highly targeted approach is known as **mass customisation**, whereby an organisation enables each customer to design a product specifically for themselves – the modern day equivalent of "bespoke" products. Usually by entering their preferred product specifications onto a web site, customers can dictate the precise styles, dimensions or functions they want from a product.

Figure 6.4

Multi-segment strategy

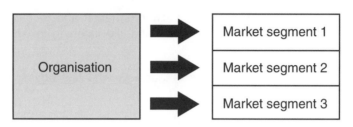

Sometimes however, an organisation – particularly one with very limited resources – is better off focusing on just one of the many market segments that exist within the overall market for a product, rather than trying to serve the interests of all the different sub-groups and individuals. This is known as **niche marketing,** and occurs when an organisation believes that it has expertise primarily in a single, narrowly defined market, and can best use its resources to address that market alone. Motor manufacturers such as Morgan Cars and Lamborghini are both examples of car producers who concentrate on serving the needs of the motoring enthusiast rather than the general public.

Figure 6.5

Concentration strategy

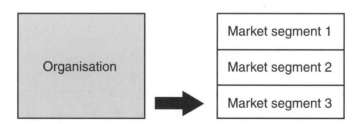

Activity 6.1 Classic segments

Research from focus groups conducted by the radio station Classic FM suggests that as much as a third of the UK population listens to classical music, but this very broad audience can be divided into five behavioural groups.

Aficionados: collectors of classical music information and recordings, who feel they are knowledgeable about music and like listening to whole works rather than snippets.

Populists: amateur classical music enthusiasts who like buying CDs, but mainly for easy listening.

Hooked on classics: tend to stick to what they know when buying music and have conservative tastes, particularly enjoying compilation CDs by famous names.

Companion listeners: like popular and recognisable classics, and enjoy listening to chart music and jazz as well as classical music on the radio.

Newcomers: are primarily familiar with pop music and culture. Regular cinema-goers who like classical music from films and adverts.

Discuss behavioural patterns in the following markets, and devise pen-portraits that describe the segments you believe make up these markets.

- Washing powder buyers.
- Mobile phone users.
- Car drivers.

Bases for market segmentation

Having decided to use a target marketing approach, an organisation is faced with the task of deciding how to group consumers together, ready to target them with marketing activity. There are four commonly used bases on which market segmentation takes place.

Geographic segmentation divides up the market based on where people live. This is often a powerful predictor of consumer needs. For example, people who live in areas where the climate is warm tend to buy more garden furniture and soft drinks than those in colder regions. Cultural norms in different countries can vary, making some products very difficult to sell. In many parts of Europe it is quite difficult to buy an electric kettle, as coffee is a much more popular drink than tea. Consumers tend to use coffee makers, and boil water far less frequently than the English. Many consumer needs, however, are common across national and regional boundaries, so more sophisticated means for dividing up markets are more common.

Activity 6.2 From little acorns...

The web site at www.caci.co.uk gives information about ACORN, a system of classifying residential neighbourhoods according to the type of person most likely to live there. From the home page menu offering "Products and Services" choose "Customer Profiling". You can download a guide to using ACORN from this area of the site. Try the associated web site at www.etypes.info to reveal a segmentation system being used to classify consumers according to their attitudes and behaviour relating to the Internet.

Also, read Hill and O'Sullivan (2004) *Foundation Marketing* (3rd Edition) FT/Prentice Hall, pages 153-167 and self-check questions 1, 4, 6, 7, and 10.

Demographic segmentation divides up the market according to people's age, gender, income, education, family life stage and other objective statistics. It is a very useful means of market segmentation, as people's product needs and usage rates vary significantly across these variables. Different generations are likely to enjoy different types of leisure activity, enjoy different holidays, listen to different music, wear different styles of clothes – so their needs have to be addressed separately. Gender can also influence product preferences. Car manufacturers have recognised that women comprise an important part of their markets, and tend to have different priorities for their vehicles, number one being safety features.

The different aspirations of different income groups also provide fertile grounds for segmentation. Mass market food retailers such as Tesco and Sainsbury's successfully meet the needs of the middle income brackets, leaving stores such as Waitrose to specialise in providing premium quality and specialist food products for those with higher disposable income, and discount stores such as Aldi to cater for those on low incomes.

Activity 6.3 Tween spirit

Go to the web site at http://www.guardian.co.uk and search under the archive section for the article entitled "What little girls are made of", by Maureen Rice, which was first published in *The Observer* on 3 December, 2000. Use this article to write a 300 word summary of the main characteristics of the market segment described as "Tweenagers" in this article.

Psychographic segmentation divides up the market based on individuals' psychological characteristics, particularly personality, social class and lifestyle. Some companies design products and services specifically to appeal to different social classes, and build in features that they know will appeal to the different social classes. Club Med provide a private resort-based cosmopolitan holiday experience, with an emphasis on sports and gourmet food. They set out to attract professional people from right across Europe, and offer them a holiday experience that is both a relaxing break from work and a stimulating and interesting environment. Other holiday clubs are aimed at less affluent segments. Such service providers tend to target holidaymakers from one country only, and emphasise the opportunity to have fun. They will provide more in terms of organised entertainment, but place less emphasis on the quality of food and accommodation. Segmentation based on lifestyle recognises that, almost regardless of income, people have widely differing values and choose to live their lives in very different ways. For example, there is a growing "environmental" segment that is very conscious of the impact of Western consumerism on the environment, and attempts to recycle and conserve scarce natural resources at every opportunity. This has led to a sizeable demand for reusable and biodegradable packaging materials. A related segment, the "health-conscious", attempts to pursue a lifestyle which respects the personal ecology of the human body: hence the growth in demand for organic foods and the popularity of brands with a reputation as "natural" products.

Behavioural segmentation divides up the market based on the ways that people respond to the products that are available. Segments can be identified which relate to the extent to which people are knowledgeable about certain products; the attitudes they have to them; the regularity with which they consume them; and the reasons they buy them.

User expertise: Some consumers are very knowledgeable about certain products. Professional photographers, for example, are likely to understand the inner workings of a camera and the desirable specification of a roll of film much better than those whose photography ambitions start and finish with holiday snaps. Consequently, the types of camera and film aimed at professional and casual photographers are very different, the former tending to emphasise quality and reliability, and the latter highlighting ease of use and price.

Benefits sought: Sometimes, different people want products for different reasons. Toothpaste provides a good example. The primary reason for buying toothpaste is obvious, to protect your teeth. But people also seek additional benefits. Some want their teeth to be whiter, some want to maintain good oral hygiene, some want to disguise bad breath, and some simply want it to taste good. The market for toothpaste is consequently very heavily segmented, with different brands aiming to deliver different benefits.

Occasion of use: People may want to use different forms of a product at different times. Ice cream can be eaten as a dessert after a meal, as a treat on the beach, during the interval at the theatre, or just sitting in an armchair in front of the telly. The market for ice cream is therefore very diverse, and its distribution reflects this – from the freezer at the supermarket, to the street vendor, the confectionery kiosk at the theatre and the cold cabinet by the checkout at the video shop.

Usage rate: Heavy users of a product may have different needs from light users. If we only buy a product from time to time, we are likely to be less price sensitive than if the product forms a major part of our weekly expenditure. Heavy users are also more receptive to joining loyalty schemes, which offer incentives and rewards for becoming regular customers.

Product attitudes: There are some people who are extremely unlikely ever to buy a certain type of product or service, as they hold very negative attitudes towards them. Segmentation based on attitudes can be very useful for identifying the people most and least likely to respond to marketing stimuli. In the arts for example theatre goers fall into four categories, known as "attenders" (those who go to the theatre regularly), "intenders" (those who like to go, but don't get around to it very often), "indifferent" (those who aren't particularly interested in theatre, but might go if someone else buys the tickets) and "hostile" (those who would not be seen dead in a theatre – like Abraham Lincoln!). Attempting to change the deeply held attitudes of the "hostile" would be too expensive and probably a fairly futile exercise, so theatres tend to use their marketing resources to target people who have been to their venues before, knowing them to be at least willing to consider buying a theatre ticket.

Activity 6.4 Give us a clue!

Research into "donor potential" is very valuable to fund-raisers, who need to know which market segments have the best potential for giving the most money. A theatre wanting to raise money for its refurbishment plans divided its customer base into four segments, relating to customers' levels of involvement with the organisation. "Attenders" had booked tickets twice in the past year; "regulars" had attended three or four times in the past year; "enthusiasts" had attended five or more times in the past year; and "friends" were members of the theatre's club. A telephone fund-raising agency ran a campaign that generated the following results.

Segment	Number of contacts	Total money pledged (4 year value (£))	Average donation (£)	Cost of campaign (£)
Attenders	229	4,000	74.74	1,145
Regulars	308	7,000	96.10	1,540
Enthusiasts	212	6,000	94.42	1,060
Friends	335	17,000	168.35	1,675

1. How much money can the theatre expect to receive over the next four years as a result of the campaign?

2. What was the average revenue per contact made in each segment?

3. How many of the enthusiasts contacted actually pledged money to the theatre?

4. What was the return on investment for the campaign in each segment? How much was it on average?

Adapted from: Salmon, A. (2001) *Journal of Arts Marketing*, Issue 1, p15.

Sometimes organisations segment their markets based on just one variable, but more commonly a range of different variables come into play. A company that is about to launch a new breakfast cereal may use geographic segmentation to concentrate on buyers in just one part of the country. But they might also use demographic segmentation, and aim at the children's market, and behavioural segmentation, aiming at parents who believe that their children should go to school with a good breakfast inside them. Similarly, holidays can be targeted at the active over 50s, families who enjoy sports, or young people with a sense of adventure – all of which are target markets that combine two segments.

Criteria for effective segmentation

For a market segment to be able to deliver a valuable customer base, it must have four important characteristics:

Size: the chosen segment must be big enough to sustain the product concerned. An organisation with low overheads and low production costs can afford to serve smaller market segments than those that have a high cost base, but there always comes a point at which the market segment is just too small to be viable. Specialist shoe manufacturers can profitably target consumers who have exceptionally large feet, but it is questionable whether anyone could make a success of targeting people with exceptionally long arms – there simply might not be enough people around who find it difficult to buy clothes with long enough sleeves.

Relevance: the chosen segment must be identified on a basis that is relevant to the market. So in the earlier example, we saw that professional photographers and amateur photographers have quite different needs, but it isn't appropriate to target that market by age or gender. These characteristics are irrelevant in the decision to purchase a camera or film.

Identify: the chosen segment should be similar to each other, but distinctly different from other segments, so that consumers in that segment understand when a product might meet their needs better than any others on the market. Consequently, organisations using age as a segmentation variable have to be careful about how they approach the market. Increasingly, youth markets are growing older at a younger age, and older people are staying younger for longer! So an organisation which targets the "over 50s" must be diplomatic in its portrayal of its chosen segment. Those aged 51 are likely to have more in common with people in their 30s and 40s than people in their 80s!

Accessibility: it must be possible to reach a chosen segment with marketing messages, and develop specific marketing programmes to meet the needs of that segment. Sometimes, a segment looks as if it holds great potential, but the logistical difficulties in reaching individuals in that segment far outweigh the benefits. University students are a good example of this. Their future value as consumers will probably be high, as they are educated to a higher level and are likely to be high-income earners in the future. However, they are widely scattered geographically and there are no major national media that consistently target them as a market segment. This makes it very difficult to influence them, other than through direct marketing techniques.

Activity 6.5 Poor students?

Students have historically been a very difficult market to target, as they are geographically scattered and relatively resistant to traditional mass media advertising techniques. However, the founders of the web site at www.hot-toast.com believe that they have come up with a formula that will break down the communication barriers to reaching this market, and are aiming to become the leading student web site. Evaluate this web site, and describe the types of student you believe would be most likely to use it. If you are a student, to what extent does it appeal to you and meet your needs? Do you think the "student" segment could be broken down further to help marketers target their communications better? If so, then what sort of sub-segments do you think exist?

Activity 6.6

CASE STUDY: Organic and functional foods

Consumer concerns over food safety, fuelled by crises such as BSE and the media's focus on GM foods, have encouraged many shoppers to seek out organic foods. Food retailers are racing to become market leaders in what promises to be one of the fastest growing sectors of the market, with sales expected to grow from £415 million in 1999 to almost £2 billion by 2010. There has, however, been resistance to becoming more organic by some of the major manufacturers, who fear that by bringing out organic versions of the foods they already produce, they are casting doubt over the ingredients of their non-organic lines.

Supply issues are also a problem with organic ingredients. The success of the organic food industry depends on both retailers and manufacturers being able to secure supplies in sufficient quantities to achieve economies of scale and reduce price premiums. There are also problems for manufacturers of processed products, such as ready meals and frozen desserts. The level of processing required for an acceptable taste may be beyond the level deemed acceptable for the product to be defined as organic.

Problems such as these have meant that some manufacturers have approached the organic market with caution. Instead, they have been busy enhancing their product lines with the introduction of "functional foods", also known as "neutriceuticals" – products that combine scientifically proven health benefits with consumer appeal. These types of food are not new. One of the earliest brands on the market was Yakult, the gut-friendly product using "good bacteria", which has been available in Japan for over 60 years but only reached the UK in 1996. Since then, the number of products that incorporate additives with proven health benefits has soared.

1999 saw the UK launch of new brands such as Benecol, the vegetable fat spread which claims to help lower cholesterol, and the Aviva range, which comprised products like fibre-rich wholemeal biscuits, digestion-aiding hot chocolate and orange juice that strengthens the bones. Distribution of Aviva products was through supermarkets, but also through health food stores and pharmacies. Clinical evidence from 160 independent global studies was put forward to support claims that the products could bring about improvements in the health of the organs concerned. The launch was based on the premise that as well as health, consumers are more than ever committed to taste, pleasure and convenience. If food does not taste good, they will not eat it. If they cannot substitute it for something they already eat on a regular basis, it will not be convenient for them to incorporate the healthier brand into their diet. Functional food has to offer a short cut to better health, without the need to develop a liking for a new taste.

After only a year on the market the parent company, Novartis, withdrew Aviva products from the UK because it was felt that the consumer proposition was not sufficiently powerful. Consumer acceptance had been slow, partly because of retailer fears over unsubstantiated health claims for the products, and partly because of the price. Faced with a choice between a well-known brand like Flora (which is not designated as a functional food, but is endorsed by a medical charity) and Benecol, which is described as a functional food but sells at a much higher price, many shoppers will still vote with their wallets.

Questions

1. To what extent is the market for organic food different from the market for functional food? What benefits do organic foods offer consumers that functional foods do not, and vice versa.

2. What type of promotional activity should be used to target potential buyers of functional foods?

Sources

'Growing appetite for health', 27 January 2000, *Marketing Week*, at www.mad.co.uk.
Harvey, J. (1999) 'Testing times for new foods', 10 June, pp38-39.
Day, J. (1999) 'Binge Benefits', 29 July, pp24-27.

SUMMARY OF KEY POINTS

-   A target marketing approach identifies the best potential market segments and attempts to meet their needs.

-   Niche marketing occurs when an organisation targets a single, narrowly defined market.

-   Markets are commonly segmented on the basis of geography, demographics, psychology and behaviour.

-   To be viable, a segment must be big enough, relevant to the consumer, different from other segments and be possible to target with marketing communications.

Glossary of terms

behavioural segmentation: dividing markets into clusters of people who react to and interact with a product in similar ways.

demographic segmentation: dividing markets into clusters of people who share a demographic characteristic, such as age, gender or income bracket.

differentiated marketing: supplying different versions of a product to give customers choice.

geographic segmentation: dividing markets into clusters of people who live in the same area.

market segmentation: the process of dividing markets into clusters of people who have similar needs for certain goods or services.

mass customisation: enabling each customer to design a product to meet their own specific requirements.

mass marketing: attempting to meet the needs of as many people as possible with a single marketing programme.

multi-segment marketing: attempting to attract a number of different market segments.

niche marketing: directing the marketing efforts of an organisation towards a single market segment.

psychographic segmentation: dividing markets into clusters of people who have a similar approach to life.

target marketing: designing complete marketing programmes to meet the needs of different segments in a market.

Self-test multiple-choice questions

1. i)   Psychographic segmentation is based on factors such as age, income and occupation.
    ii) Niche marketing is the process of targeting a psychographic segment.

    Which of these is true?
    a)   i only.
    b)   ii only.
    c)   both i and ii.
    d)   neither i nor ii.

2. **Which two of the following are examples of behavioural segmentation?**
    a)   Segmentation based on occasion of use.
    b)   Segmentation based on country of birth.
    c)   Segmentation based on benefits sought.
    d)   Segmentation based on family size.

3. **Which of the following is NOT a criterion for a worthwhile market segment?**
    a)   Identifiably different from other market segments.
    b)   Big enough to sustain profitable business.
    c)   Within a clearly defined geographic area.
    d)   Relevant to product benefit.

4. **Which one of the following marketing approaches allows large numbers of customers to specify individual products?**
    a)   Mass marketing.
    b)   Niche marketing.
    c)   Differentiated marketing.
    d)   Mass customisation.

5. **Geographic segmentation could be based on which two of the following.**
    a)   Regions that have a similar climate.
    b)   Countries that share the same language.
    c)   Consumer beliefs about environmental issues.
    d)   Patterns of population growth.

Something to think about...

1. To what extent do colleges and universities segment their markets?

2. Compare the marketing approaches of Ford Motor Company and Morgan Cars.

3. How many segments can you identify in the market for dog food?

4. Why does no one market cameras for tall people? Bicycles for students? Single (as opposed to pairs of) socks?

5. On what bases is the market for national newspapers segmented?

Session 7

Product – what's on offer?

Product is possibly the single most important element of the marketing mix. This Session introduces you to the basic ideas behind product analysis and explores how products need to change to keep pace with consumer needs.

LEARNING OUTCOMES

By the end of this Session you should be able to:

- Appreciate the difference between features and benefits when it comes to products and services.

- Describe and illustrate the main stages of the product life cycle.

- Demonstrate understanding of the dimensions of product mix (width and depth).

- Explain and justify the process of branding.

STUDY TEXT

What is a product?

A **product** is anything that is offered by an organisation or individual to satisfy a customer need. That is a pretty broad definition! As a customer, a product can be anything you find useful and exchange something of value for. So the term not only covers the kinds of product you buy at the supermarket (such as food, detergent or toilet tissue) but also things like electricity, gas, television programmes, telephone services, pop stars, even ideas. Some would even go so far as to describe religions and political parties as products. Certainly politicians are not novices when it comes to marketing! The term "product" is usually used interchangeably with the term "physical goods" to differentiate it from the concept of a service (whose characteristics we will explore in Session 11). The broad definition, however, allows a product to be a service too!

Features and benefits

Features are the attributes of a product – what it looks like, how many knobs it has, its technical specifications. Benefits are what it actually does for the customer. Customers do not buy features – they buy benefits.

Activity 7.1 The benefit in question

Here is a selection of products with some example features listed against each one. Find someone in your tutor group, family or workplace, who uses one or more of the products and interview them to find out what benefits they are looking for from the products.

Product	Features (Examples only. Yours may be different.)	Benefits
Breakdown Recovery Service	■ Recovery of driver plus four passengers. ■ Covers one hour's labour, plus parts up to £100 if fault is repairable at roadside. ■ Guaranteed to reach you in 60 minutes or £10 refund.	
Television	■ NICAM stereo sound. ■ 22 inch screen. ■ Integrated DVD player. ■ Teletext.	
Mobile Telephone	■ Extended battery life. ■ Voice-activated dialling. ■ Vibration alert. ■ Picture Messaging. ■ Miniature size. ■ Selection of games and ring tones. ■ Changeable covers.	
Dental Check-up	■ Examination. ■ Discussion with dentist. ■ Polish and scale.	

As you have worked through this exercise, it may have struck you that different customers want different benefits, which might even come from the same feature on a product. For example, a business traveller might want a tiny mobile phone because of its portability, whereas a dedicated follower of fashion might covet the same object because it is the last word in chic. This is why the concept of "benefits-sought" segmentation is of such interest to marketers. Knowing what different groups of customers want from your product lets you decide how best to market it.

The distinction between features and benefits is one of the most valuable ideas marketing has to offer. It helps you see things through the customer's eyes. The danger for any organisation is to see its products in terms of features and forget about the benefits that customers are actually after. Marketing history is littered with the remains of companies whose view of their business was so narrowly focused on features that they did not notice when their customers started finding more effective benefits elsewhere.

Really successful products in the long term have a **Unique Selling Proposition** – something about them that confers benefits unobtainable from any other product on the market. Top-flight marketing involves constant vigilance to ensure that the Unique Selling Proposition (USP) is kept relevant to the target market by continuous product improvement and refinement.

Analysing a product

Thinking about features and benefits leads us to a more formal way of looking at products and what they offer customers: product analysis. We can use this technique to look at any product in order to discover ways of making it more attractive to target customers. As an illustration we will analyse a familiar product, an automatic washing machine. Washing machines are a good example of what marketing calls **consumer durables.** These are products like cars, hi-fi's and kitchen appliances that we buy for our own use and that of our families (hence "consumer"), but expect to last for several years (hence "durables").

Figure 7.1

The Total Product Concept

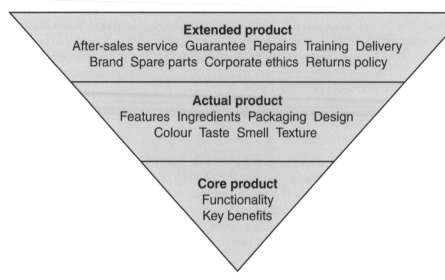

There are a number of approaches to product analysis. A simple and effective one portrays three "levels" of product (Figure 7.1) as three layers. At the most fundamental level is the **core product** – the satisfaction of a genuine customer need. In this case it is the simple but valuable benefit of having clean clothes with a minimum of effort.

The next level is the **actual product,** the product's features. These include appearance, taste, size, styling, weight, format, packaging – all the tangible aspects of a product that you can think of, and which manufacturers can mix and match to suit the target market. For a washing machine, features might include spin speed, number and types of washing programmes and power consumption figures. These features can all confer benefits. The size of the wash drum will dictate the number of clothes you can wash at one time. The key is to make the features relevant to the benefits sought by your target groups, otherwise you are simply building in features that make the product more confusing or expensive than it needs to be. Beware the temptation to be product-oriented. Marketing is about customer-orientation.

The third level is what we call the **extended product.** This describes the halo of less tangible attributes surrounding the immediate product. They include guarantees, branding, service, delivery – the things that add value to the basic product. For a washing machine the extended product will include the warranty, delivery arrangements, installation, the instruction manual, and the manufacturers reputation or brand.

Product analysis helps marketing managers understand the core benefits that customers are seeking and tweak the actual and extended aspects of their products to satisfy them exactly. Marketing executives are often called brand managers or product managers to reflect this central role of manipulating the product to suit the needs of the customer.

Activity 7.2 Design matters

Product design is one of the ways in which manufacturers communicate the benefits of their products to potential customers. Using the Internet, download at least three product images and insert them in a word processed document, writing brief notes on each as to why the product design or packaging is appropriate to the target market. A convenient way of downloading images is simply to click on them using your right hand mouse button. This presents you with a pop-up menu which should offer you an option to save the image, such as "Save Picture As" (the precise words will depend on which browser you are using). Take this option and then follow the dialogue box to save to an appropriate directory/folder. You can then use the "Insert" command from your word processor (taking the Picture and From File options if available from subsequent drop-down menus).

Product life cycle

Customer needs do not stand still, and products that don't change with the times tend to get left behind. Technological and social developments conspire to alter customer expectations. What we see as a luxury in one generation of products becomes a basic requirement in the next (central locking on cars for example). This means that products inevitably become outdated, to be replaced by newer, more effective ways of satisfying customer needs. In one sense this acts in the best interests of everyone – as manufacturers compete to outdo one another in quality and performance. In another sense it can be depressing, as you watch your once top-of-the range computer becoming a virtual antique in a matter of years because of the speed of technological change in the IT market.

The model of the Product Life Cycle (PLC) helps us to understand the process of change by suggesting that all products go through recognisable stages, from launch to decline. The interesting thing about the PLC is that we can recognise clear marketing priorities at each stage of the life cycle. Such priorities dictate the kind of activity marketing managers use to support their products.

New products are constantly appearing on the market to satisfy what marketers see as potentially profitable needs. These products may have taken several years and a great deal of money to develop. The launch stage sees their sponsors, like anxious new parents, working overtime to ensure the successful entry into the world of their offspring. Loving attention is lavished on the new product launch in the shape of promotion and distribution. A fortune may be spent on getting consumers to try the unfamiliar new brand (e.g. free samples through letterboxes, money-back or buy-one-get-one-free offers in supermarkets). At the same time manufacturers will be desperately seeking shelf space to guarantee maximum exposure to the buying public. Key retailers are courted with promises of saturation advertising and hefty discounts.

Figure 7.2

The product life cycle

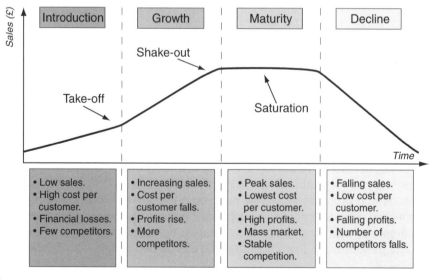

At launch stage, in spite of the best efforts of energetic and talented marketers, a lot of products come to grief. Those that survive this high-risk stage go on to the next phase: growth. The effort to widen distribution continues, in order to find new outlets for the product. Advertising support is still important, but the emphasis is on stimulating word of mouth to build on existing success and draw in more new users. If the product is ahead of its competition and offers benefits that cannot be obtained elsewhere, high prices can be justified. On the other hand, marketing expenses are likely to be high as well, so the level of profit is limited until the product gathers its own momentum.

Competitors are quick to pick up on new markets as they emerge. Soon even the most original products will have imitators as competitors. As these "me-too" products enter the fray, the market eventually becomes saturated and stops growing. This ushers in the third stage of the PLC: maturity. At the approach of middle age, the product slows down. To keep the customer interested, promotional effort now turns to short-term sales promotions as well as longer-term reminder advertising. By now, manufacturing processes will have become much more efficient than they were at launch and growth. The resulting cost-savings make the business more profitable, but also fuel price-cutting to consumers (which becomes more important as competition increases). Distribution is now more or less established, but occasionally new customer segments can be addressed through new outlets – such as selling financial services through supermarkets.

In spite of the fact that the maturity stage is usually the longest phase in the life cycle of a product, and can be refreshed by relaunches and imaginative tactics, sooner or later a product declines. Demand falls off, perhaps because of a widespread social change. Sometimes this decline stage is extremely sudden. The paper-based Encyclopaedia Britannica almost went out of business in 1999 because of the sudden popularity of CD-ROM competitors, and has had to relaunch itself as an online service to stay afloat.

Activity 7.3 A new lease of life?

One of the most fruitful ways of extending a product's life cycle is to find a new use for it. Examples include using breakfast cereals as cooking ingredients, incorporating chocolate bars, such as Cadbury's Flake, into ice creams, and pipecleaners as craft materials. Working with at least two other people, brainstorm some new uses for a product with which you are all familiar. Appoint someone to write the ideas on a flip chart. Don't criticise ideas for the first five minutes, just try to come up with as many as possible. Then try to pick the best three. It may be that the illogical ideas suggest more plausible ones once you start selecting!

Think of brand names and an advertising strap line or slogan for each which reflects the kind of market you might aim to target.

Product mix

Most successful companies do not rely on just one product, but have a number of different products (often at different stages of the life cycle). Products in the mature and decline stages help support the ones still in the earlier stages. Another advantage of having a variety of products is it helps spread the risk. Rather than putting all your eggs in one basket, having a number of products in the market helps protect against fluctuations in demand and allows access to more than one market segment.

Lever Brothers manufactures a number of different products for clothes and household cleaning. These products are classic examples of what marketing calls **fast-moving consumer goods.** They are the staple fare of supermarket shopping – things we buy regularly, use up, and then buy again. This makes them fast-moving (as they move quickly through the trade to the end-user), and they are consumer goods because people like us buy them for our own use and that of our families.

Lever Brothers' total range of products, cleaners, detergents, washing-up liquid, in all their sizes and varieties, is called their **product mix.** A product mix contains a number of **product lines,** families of products of a particular type, for example clothes-washing detergents. Marketing terminology uses the image of width and depth to describe the number of product lines overall, and the number of varieties within each product line. The more product lines a company offers (household cleaning line, detergent line, personal care line, etc.) the greater the **width** of its product mix. The more varieties within each product line (e.g. different brands of detergent), the greater the **depth** of its product mix.

Activity 7.4 Mind mapping product

If you've never tried spider diagrams, pattern notes or mind mapping (three names for the same thing) as a note-taking technique, this exercise will give you the opportunity. If you already use the technique, perhaps this will give you a few more ideas on how to improve on it.

Apparently our brains remember things by making connections – literally. Spider diagrams allow us to incorporate that organic process into our own learning techniques. Doing a spider diagram of the concept of product is a good starting point for seeing if the technique works for you.

Take an A4 sheet of paper and lay it out landscape way round on the desk. Try and find a number of different coloured pens. In the middle of the paper write the word Product – or perhaps draw a little picture that reminds you of it (I always think of a Kit Kat!). Following the sections in this Session, or using the fuller account of Product in Chapter 7 of the course text (Hill and O'Sullivan (2004) *Foundation Marketing* (3rd Edition) FT/Prentice Hall, pages 178-182, 188-197 and 199-205), draw branch lines out from the middle word or image to represent product analysis, product range, product life cycle and branding. Label each of these branches, and from each one draw sub branches to represent the themes and information under each subheading. Add little diagrams, cartoons and examples. Use colour to help make the material memorable. If it looks messy don't worry – the point is to be useful rather than win the Turner Prize!

Try putting the finished spider diagram where you will see it regularly. The bathroom door is a good place. It should now contain all you need to know about product. Once you've looked at it a few times you should be able to visualise it in your mind – and you will be a walking expert on product theory!

You can make other spider diagrams based on the other Sessions, and even build up a mega spider diagram to link some of the ideas about marketing that you find most useful.

Brands

At its most basic, a **brand** is the manufacturer's stamp that marks out a product as the work of a particular producer. This identity is the focus for the reputation of the product in the minds of its customers. If they are satisfied with it, they will ask for it again. Branding therefore works in the interests of customers by guaranteeing quality and consistency in goods and services. It works in the interests of manufacturers by allowing them to build customer loyalty. Trademark law means that companies can defend their brands from imitators, so that the customer can be sure of the genuine article.

Organisations can enhance their brands' reputations in a number of ways. Investing in research and development aimed at quality improvement is one way. Advertising and promotion in order to polish the brand's image is another. The expense of this process has led to criticisms of branding, saying it leads to higher prices than need be. Manufacturers argue, however, that quality always comes at a price. You get what you pay for in life. Less famous names, or supermarket "own label" brands, while offering temporary savings for consumers, can represent poor value in the long term because of poor performance.

Heinz Tomato Ketchup, Andrex Toilet Tissue and Gordon's Gin are all examples of brands which are more expensive than unbranded rival products, but which lead their markets because of quality and value.

Activity 7.5 Value for money

The next time you are in a large supermarket make a note of the price of the most expensive and least expensive brands in the following product categories. (You can do this as a group by each looking at a different category, and then sharing the information). In order to be able to compare prices on a like-for-like basis, make sure you note what the pack size or weight is in each case.

- Instant Coffee.
- Tea Bags.
- Toilet Tissue.
- Tomato Ketchup.
- Baked Beans.

Now set out a table indicating the grams per penny for each product. What is the percentage difference in grams per penny between the two varieties in each case?

Activity 7.6

CASE STUDY: Scrabbling for success

Scrabble, the world's most popular word game, dates from the 1930s. New owner Mattel, a leading toy and games company operating internationally, decided in 1998 that it was time for a fresh look at the brand. The company felt that the rules and basic format of the game were fine. Certainly its enduring popularity, second only to Monopoly in the board game stakes, suggested that to tinker with the principles of the game itself would not be a good idea. Indeed sales had gone up in recent years. However, in the face of increased competition for in-home entertainment from video, DVD and computer games, the image of the game needed refreshing. A product design agency was briefed to look at every aspect of the presentation, from the style of the lettering on the tiles to the colour and material of the bag in which they are kept.

Market research suggested that Scrabble, although still a strong brand, was indeed seen as a little old-fashioned by potential and actual customers. The designers working on the project were paid to play the game in order to get to know it inside out. Qualitative research was carried out with a sample of 5,000 existing players. The findings identified six player segments, from "family entertainers" to "serious game players". The benefit they all looked for in common from the game was fun and intellectual challenge – so a positioning of "convivial mental sparring" was chosen for the game.

The result of the project was a new-look Scrabble for the new millennium. The box remained green (plans to relaunch it in red were overturned by Mattel as being too sharp a break with the past), the logo was made to look like a tile itself, with newly designed lettering which also appeared on the playing pieces, and the old strap line ("The world's leading word game") was replaced by the snappier "Every word counts". Inside the box the board had a new surface that helped tiles stick. Furthermore, there are plans to bring out online and PlayStation versions of the game. Sales of the relaunched version of Scrabble Original as it is now called, have been reassuring, with increases of over 30% in some key markets.

Questions

1. Draw a Total Product Concept diagram for Scrabble Original. Do you agree that the core benefit is "convivial mental sparring"?

2. How can you relate the theory of the Product Life Cycle to the relaunch of Scrabble as Scrabble Original?

3. What barriers might Scrabble Original face in the international marketplace? How might Mattel go about overcoming them?

Sources

Company Information, Buxton, P. (2001) 'How to keep favour with old favourites', *Marketing,* 4th January, pp21-22.

SUMMARY OF KEY POINTS

-   A good product is fundamental to successful marketing.

-   Features are the attributes of a product, like taste, weight, smell and quality. But they are only the means to an end – bestowing benefits on consumers.

-   Product Life Cycle portrays products as being born, growing, maturing and declining (just like the people who buy them).

-   Companies tend to offer a range of products in order to spread their risk and smooth out cash flow.

-   Brands are products that are unique to an identified manufacturer. Branding allows manufacturers to build customer loyalty.

Glossary of terms

actual product: the tangible features of a product which deliver benefits to the customer.

benefits: the advantages a buyer anticipates from buying a product or service.

brand: a product which belongs uniquely to one producer.

consumer durables: products designed for use over a period of time.

core product: the basic function of a product which satisfies customer needs.

depth of product mix: the number of items in a product line.

extended product: intangible features of a product which provide additional psychological benefits to the customer.

Fast-Moving Consumer Goods (FMCGs): household products which are bought on a regular basis.

features: the characteristics that distinguish one product or brand from another.

product life cycle: a four-stage model (Introduction, Growth, Maturity, Decline) for describing the common sales patterns that can be observed over the lifetime of a product.

product line: a group of closely related products sold by an organisation.

product mix: the total set of all product items sold by an organisation.

total product concept: the combination of tangible and intangible attributes of a product which combine to offer benefits to the customer.

Unique Selling Proposition (USP): the feature, unique to any successful long-term product, which differentiates it from any of its competitors.

width of product mix: the number of different product lines a firm sells.

Self-test multiple-choice questions

1. **Which one of the following features of a product is an aspect of the extended product?**
    a) Packaging.
    b) Size.
    c) Texture.
    d) Warranty.

2. **Which of the following attributes of a computer is a benefit rather than a feature?**
   a) Processor speed.
   b) Memory size.
   c) Pre-installed software.
   d) Ease of use.

3. **Which of the following stages of the product life cycle is usually the longest stage?**
   a) Decline.
   b) Maturity.
   c) Growth.
   d) Launch.

4. **The number of different varieties within a product line is referred to as...**
   a) The product mix height.
   b) The product mix depth.
   c) The product mix width.
   d) The product mix length.

5. **Branding can be seen to act in the interests of customers by...**
   a) Raising prices.
   b) Guaranteeing quality and consistency.
   c) Building customer loyalty.
   d) Shortening product life cycles.

Something to think about...

1. What potential benefits might the following products offer to consumers of different ages? Confectionery, cars, clothes, bank accounts, holidays, stationery.

2. Draw a Total Product Concept diagram analysing a product you use at home or at work. Suggest one way in which the product could be improved by changes at the actual and/or extended level.

3. Illustrate the product life cycle using examples from a particular market sector such as confectionery or motor cars.

4. How (if at all) does the product life cycle account for the following? Computer games, designer clothes, mobile telephones.

5. What are the advantages and disadvantages of having a wide product mix?

Session 8

Price – the value that customers exchange for benefits

Price is the one element of the marketing mix that generates income rather than costs. This Session outlines the essential influences on setting prices and points out how different approaches to pricing can support a range of marketing aims.

LEARNING OUTCOMES

At the end of this Session you should be able to:

- Describe and illustrate a range of pricing tactics aimed at making sales more profitable or at increasing sales volume.

- Perform simple calculations aimed at discovering break-even point and price elasticity of demand.

- Identify influences on pricing – including costs, customer expectations and competitor behaviour.

STUDY TEXT

Price

Price decisions are crucial to marketing success. Charge too much and you will lose customers, but charge too little and you may go out of business. As an element of the marketing mix, Price has a close relationship with each of the other three Ps. It is tied to Product quality (you tend to get what you pay for), Place/distribution (customers may be prepared to trade convenience for lower prices) and Promotion (advertising can often help maintain higher prices). It is therefore important to consider the marketing mix as a whole when trying to understand an organisation's pricing policy.

Costs are an obvious starting point in any consideration of pricing, but, as we shall see, they are by no means the whole story. There are a number of more general factors, both external and internal, that are worth thinking about as we introduce the subject. First of all, an organisation's own resources may dictate what kind of pricing it can afford. Organisations that are cash rich are taking less of a gamble if they charge high prices. If the higher prices mean slower sales, it is not the end

123

of the world as the organisation's need for cash flow is not desperate. On the other hand, an organisation with poor cash flow might need to stimulate income as a matter of urgency through low prices from the word go.

External factors are another important consideration. In times of expansion and high consumer demand, prices have a natural tendency to rise. This results in inflation, which governments try to control by making credit more expensive. As interest rates go up however, businesses have less incentive to produce new goods, and concentrate instead on selling off their existing stocks – often at a discount. The resulting low prices are meant to stimulate demand, in order to get the economy expanding again. While these movements in the economic environment are beyond the control of any individual business, it is nevertheless worth taking into account the general economic climate when making pricing decisions. The "feel-good factor", also known as business and consumer confidence, can mean that customers are less concerned about high prices than they might be in less prosperous times.

Activity 8.1 What's it worth?

Discuss this with one or two other students.

How much are you prepared to pay for water in the following situations?

- As a personal spray on a hot day?

- As ice cubes from an off licence?

- In a bottle from a supermarket?

- In a bottle in a nightclub or pub?

- In the minibar of a hotel fridge on a foreign trip?

- Out of the tap?

If you can't agree on a definite price each time, see if you can at least sort these various presentations of H_2O into an agreed order, based on how much they would cost.

Pricing for profit

Pricing tactics that aim to maximise profit try to exact the highest price the market is prepared to pay. Often this means that only a small segment of the market will actually buy the product, but they are prepared to pay over the odds for their purchases. **Price skimming** is a common tactic in industries (such as business software) where innovation is important to customers, but where suppliers need to protect the investment they have made in research and development. The image is from skimming the cream off a pint of milk (in the days when milk came with cream!). In other words, the market is segmented by ability to pay and only the top segment is targeted. As competitors enter the market prices naturally fall, but by then – at least theoretically – the innovators will have recouped their outlay.

Premium pricing is a similar idea, but here the aim is to maintain the high price permanently on a particular product, perhaps as part of a manufacturer's range or as one of a number of choices in a market. We can see this kind of pricing at work in the grocery market. Everyday brands form the bulk of purchases, but an important part of grocery profits come from premium brands bought for special occasions (such as seasonal food) or simply as the occasional treat.

Differential pricing is a pricing technique that charges different groups of customers different prices. It can be used for a number of reasons, but one is to maximise the potential revenue from a market where customers can be segmented by their willingness or ability to pay. Theatres are a good example of this. Clearly, a limited number of their audience are very well off, and consider going to the theatre or opera as an opportunity to display their wealth. At the other end of the scale are low-income groups such as pensioners and students who fancy a budget night out, but would not consider high prices. Charging different prices for different seats allows theatres to soak the rich and get as much out of the less well off as they are prepared to pay.

Auction is a traditional form of pricing which has received a new lease of life thanks to Internet companies such as eBay.com. As in the standard auction, buyers bid for goods and the highest bid is accepted. This means that the purchaser is effectively setting his or her own price (although the seller is not obliged to accept it if it is not considered high enough). The advantage of auction as a form of pricing is that it gives the seller the assurance that the maximum available price at that particular time has been achieved. The disadvantage however is that there is a certain amount of unpredictability in the amount raised.

Pricing for volume (penetration pricing, discounting)

The laws of supply and demand suggest that the cheaper the price of a good or service, the more will be demanded. This is true up to a point (there is a limit for example to the amount of doughnuts you are likely to want to buy at any price!), but generally, if manufacturers want to achieve high volume sales they charge low prices.

Penetration pricing is the opposite of skimming. Instead of going for a few well-heeled customers, it tries to reach as many as possible by offering rock-bottom prices. It is usually associated with companies trying to establish themselves quickly in existing markets. A foreign competitor making an entry into a national market might well choose this route. There are a number of points to bear in mind however about this form of pricing. First of all, it is not worth using penetration pricing unless you are sure the market is expanding. It is hardly worth buying share in a shrinking market. Secondly, companies who use penetration pricing need plenty of manufacturing capacity. If the point of low prices is to sell lots of a product, the company needs to be able to supply the demand created. The third condition is that your organisation should have enough resources to be able to cope with any cash flow problems that might arise from undercutting the competition. It may be some time before the company reaps the benefits of such an aggressive strategy.

Discounting also offers low prices as a route to volume. Here the low prices are tied to a specific period of time for a particular customer or group of customers. Discounting can, for example, be conditional on a customer buying more than might normally be expected in a single transaction, like with the "three for the price of two" offers. Whether such offers increase volumes overall or just bring forward business that would have happened anyway is open to question. It is likely that the answer to the question depends on which sector you are looking at. Buying more disposable nappies in one go is unlikely to increase one's overall consumption of them. The same cannot be said of cream cakes however!

Activity 8.2 Picturing price

Research suggests that we all have a preferred way of connecting with the world through our senses. Some people are most comfortable with receiving information through hearing. They "like the sound" of an idea. Others get more physically involved with taking in information. They like to "weigh up" ideas, and have a "gut feeling" about things. A third group are happiest with the visual dimension. They like "the look" of something, they "see what you mean". We all use all three systems of receiving information and ideas, but we tend to prefer one.

Being aware of our preferences can help us become more effective learners. It means that we can actively seek out learning opportunities that are in the system we are most comfortable with, and make a more conscious effort to develop our sensitivity to other systems when we don't have a choice. So if we are good at hearing information, lectures and discussions are powerful learning opportunities. For the more physically oriented, role-playing exercises and case studies work well. And for the visually gifted, diagrams are an invaluable resource.

The visual dimension is the focus of this exercise. This Session features two graphs (Figure 8.1 on break-even analysis and Figure 8.2 on price elasticity of demand). If you are comfortable with visual representation, graphs like these provide a valuable learning resource. Diagrams of any sort can be extremely helpful – both in learning and communicating what we know. This exercise asks you to conceive and draw three simple diagrams to explain the following concepts.

- Price skimming.
- Penetration pricing.
- Differential pricing.

If you find this a useful exercise in improving your own learning, try to find opportunities to draw diagrams as you study other Sessions and the course text. Be sure to get the maximum benefit from your textbooks by studying any diagrams or charts in them carefully. Look out for the ones in the material on price in Hill and O'Sullivan (2004) *Foundation Marketing* (3rd Edition) FT/Prentice Hall, paying particular attention to pages 235-258 and pages 73-79 and self-check questions 3, 4, 6 and 13.

Cost influences on price (fixed and variable costs: break-even analysis)

Without a reasonably accurate idea of how much it costs to produce your goods or services, it is difficult to know where to start with setting a price. Unfortunately, costs are not quite as straightforward to assess as they might appear. Each product in a range has to be systematically costed in order to understand its individual contribution to overall profitability. The situation becomes even more complex when attempting to establish costs in service industries as, by their very nature, services are more difficult to quantify than physical goods.

There are two types of costs: fixed and variable. **Fixed costs** (also known as indirect costs or overheads) remain the same irrespective of the volume of goods produced. They include things like rent and wages for permanent employees. **Variable costs** (also known as direct costs) go up or down (vary) with the volume of goods produced. They include things like ingredients and raw materials.

Fixed costs and variable costs added together make total costs. Armed with a knowledge of your total costs, you can make a stab at working out what price you need to charge your customers to cover your costs and generate a profit. A word of warning however. While this approach is fine in theory, in practice it can be very difficult to establish fixed or variable costs precisely over a period of time. This is why organisations need clear accounting conventions to prevent confusion or conflict over which costs get set against which products.

Break-even analysis is a simple technique that allows marketers to work out the point at which the income from selling a product will equal the costs of making it – in other words, the break-even point. Of course the income from sales will depend on how many units are sold and at what price. This means that you can try out a number of different potential prices in your calculations and go with the one that you feel is most likely to be successful. Here your judgement will be guided by your experience with this or a similar product in the past, and by the other aspects of your marketing mix.

Figure 8.1

Break-even analysis

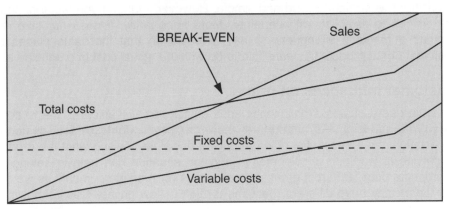

The relationship can be represented on a graph, or by a simple mathematical formula. For the formula you calculate the fixed costs associated with the product, and then divide this figure by the difference between the individual selling price of the product and how much it costs (in variable costs) to make each unit. This will give you the number of units you need to sell in order to cover your costs and make a profit.

We can express the formula as follows:

Break-even Point = Fixed Costs/(Selling Price - Variable Costs Per Unit)

Activity 8.3 Sounds profitable?

Break-even analysis can be undertaken using the given formula or by drawing a graph. Create your own graph to solve this problem. You can use Figure 8.1 as a model.

Expected sales of a new CD are set at 10,000 units at £12 each. The fixed costs of production are £31,500 and the variable costs are £7.50 per unit. Calculate how many CDs need to be sold before breaking even. How much profit will the manufacturer make if the expected sales materialise?

Cost-plus pricing is closely related to break-even analysis. Having worked out the total costs of an individual product, a percentage profit is added, like a mark-up, to achieve the final selling price. In many ways this is an attractive approach to pricing. It is straightforward and simple. However it ignores the fact that costs are difficult to establish with certainty. More importantly, it does not take into account a market's willingness to pay. It could be that the value placed by customers on a product has very little to do with the actual cost of producing it.

Customer influences on price

Marketing as a business philosophy sees customer satisfaction as the route to long-term success. As marketers therefore, we ought to see customer expectations as an essential guide to pricing decisions. Asking what the product or service is worth to a customer in a given situation can help in setting an appropriate price. Different groups of customers (or market segments as we can call them) may have different reactions to high or low prices. This is known as **price sensitivity:** the degree to which a customer is deterred by higher prices. Customers' price sensitivity tends to be greater in markets where purchases are frequent and there are a number of different suppliers from which to choose, such as petrol.

A related concept is **price elasticity of demand.** Borrowed from economics, this useful concept attempts to measure the resilience of demand for a product in the face of fluctuations in price. The image the concept uses is of an imaginary rubber band, connecting the level of demand for a product with its price level. Some goods and services display what is known as inelastic demand. Here the rubber band does not stretch very much if the price goes up. In such cases demand either remains the same or decreases to a lesser extent than the percentage increase in price. Typical markets where this is true are essential services such as gas or electricity. In markets where we have more discretion over whether or not to purchase, elastic demand is demonstrated. Here the imaginary rubber band is very stretchy indeed, with demand decreasing to a greater extent than the percentage increase in price. Luxury goods, foreign holidays and live entertainment are all vulnerable sectors to this effect.

Because conditions vary from market to market, and between market segments, it is hard to make generalisations about price elasticity of demand. It is, however, a very useful piece of information within a specific market when contemplating the likely effect of a price change, or in deciding what an appropriate price for a new product might be. The calculation again takes the form of a simple formula, which can also be expressed as a graph.

Price elasticity of demand = % Change in Quantity Demanded/% Change in Price.

If the resulting figure is greater than one, demand is deemed relatively elastic. In other words the change in sales volume is greater, proportionally, than the change in price. If the figure is one or less than one, demand is deemed relatively inelastic. In this case demand is less affected by the price going up or down, and the change in the volume of sales is proportionally smaller than the change in price. By the way, for the purposes of this calculation we do not have to worry about directed numbers (i.e. numbers which have minus or plus signs in front of them) as changes in either demand or price can be negative or positive but still display a correlation.

Figure 8.2

Price elasticity of demand

% change in demand/% change in price

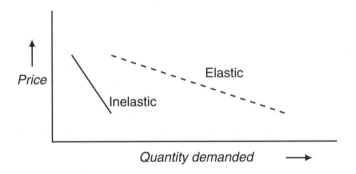

Quantity demanded

Activity 8.4 Elasticity exercise

Using the given formula, work out the price elasticity demand of the following products.

Price elasticity of demand = % Change in Quantity Demanded/% Change in Price.

a) Terrikin Fruit Puddings Cherry Snow: a frozen family dessert.

In 1999 sold 15,000 units at £1.35 each.
In 2000 sold 14,000 units at £1.45 each.

b) Nuxalot Biscuits: a luxury dog biscuit assortment with nuts and raisins for that special companion in your life.

In 1999 sold 33,000 bags at £1.50.
In 2000 sold 31,500 bags at £1.60.

c) Solarspot Holidays: a package holiday company specialising in short breaks for the over 60s.

In 1999 sold 14,000 holidays at an average price of £850.
In 2000 sold 12,000 holidays at an average price of £920.

Once you've done the basic calculation you might want to reflect on what the figures say about the price sensitivity of customers in each market. One reason why buyers are prepared to tolerate higher prices is when a product has little or no competition. Can you think of any further examples where this might be the case?

Activity 8.5 What if?

Break-even analysis and other forms of calculation aimed at price decisions are made easy by using spreadsheets. Try using Microsoft Excel's Scenario function to simplify the process. This exercise assumes prior knowledge of the basics of a spreadsheet like Excel, and access to a copy of Excel 5.0 or above.

1. Set up a spreadsheet as follows for a product where you have calculated your Fixed Costs as £150,000 and the Variable Cost per unit as £3.73. You can use your own values, but these are illustrative.

	A	B
1	Fixed costs	150,000
2	Variable costs	3.73
3		
4	Selling price	
5		
6	Break-even point	= (B1/(B4-B2))

Label a cell (here it's A4) as "Selling Price".

Label another cell (here it's A6) as "Break-even point" and enter a formula that reproduces the break-even formula we have covered earlier in the Session. The original formula is Break-even point = Fixed Costs/(Selling Price - Variable Cost per Unit). That translates, according to the positions of the relevant cells in this spreadsheet, to: = (B1/(B4-B2)).

The value you will see here at first is nonsensical, or you might get an error message, because of the fact that B4 is currently blank.

2. Now use the Scenario function to suggest a range of prices for the product and see at the touch of a button what the resulting break-even values are.

First click on the Tools option on the menu bar running across the top of the spreadsheet. Then choose Scenarios from the drop-down menu that appears. It's about halfway down the list on the standard set up for the program.

3. Clicking on Scenarios will bring up a dialogue box called "Scenario Manager". This contains a message pointing out that no scenarios have been defined (you are, in fact about to define one) and asks you to add one.

4. Click on the Add button, and another dialogue box will appear called "Add Scenario".

5. Enter "Price at £5 each" in the Scenario Name field. Then specify B4 as the Changing Cell in the appropriate field. There is a Comment field at the bottom of the dialogue box that should automatically contain information on when and by whom the scenario has been created. Clicking on OK will bring up the Scenario Values dialogue box. Specify the value of £5 for cell B4 for this scenario.

6. Clicking OK will lead to the Scenario Manager dialogue box reappearing. Go through steps 4 and 5 above with two more scenarios named "Price at £6 each" and "Price at £7 each", with 6 and 7 as the respective values for B4.

> 7. You will notice that the Scenario Manager dialogue box now lists each of the three scenarios you have created. In order to show the effect of each selling price on the break-even figure, highlight the relevant title and click on the button marked "Show". The values shown in B6 will change for each of the scenarios. At a price of £5 it will be 118,110, at £6 it will be 66,079 and at £7 it will be 45,872.
>
> Saving the spreadsheet will save the scenarios with it.
>
> Clearly this is a simple scenario, and you can imagine how it might be built up to a much more complex set of interlinked possibilities with a greater number of changeable values.

Activity 8.6

CASE STUDY: Currying favour?

Thomson, the hotel and travel agent holiday group, has almost a third of the UK holiday market. Recently in the face of price-cutting by its competitors, it launched an advertising campaign to try and move the focus of competition from price to quality. The advertisements, created by the agency responsible for the controversial "Tango" campaigns, featured a scene in an airport lounge where a passenger accuses another man of being a sadist for taking his wife on a cut-price holiday – saving precisely £20. "Surely that man's wife deserves to go with Thomson" he exclaims (to applause from the crowd that has gathered). "Would you risk the love of this fine woman for the price of a curry?"

The message is that Thomson holidays might cost a little more but offer an experience that is smoother and more enjoyable at every stage. Even the idea of setting the ad in an airport lounge rather than a sun drenched beach or poolside (where most holiday advertising seems to take place) was to make a subtle point about the difference a good holiday company makes to the tedious details of a holiday.

The company bases its strategy on the conviction that a holiday is one of the most important purchases made by anyone during the year. This being the case, value for money should be much more important than crude price advantage. But, in the age of the Internet, holidaymakers are better informed about travel bargains than ever before. As a way of comparing prices and availability it is unrivalled. The Internet may even be threatening the service difference that Thomson is stressing at point of sale. Rival operator Thomas Cook now has web terminals in most of its high street branches for customer use. It claims that a strong web presence has helped it access a new market. 50% of visitors to the thomascook.com site in its launch year had never booked with the company before.

The web is popular with budget travellers as well. The vast majority of easyJet's business is done from its web site. Furthermore, easyJet is one of a number of "no frills" airlines that are having remarkable success in luring passengers away from traditional carriers. It would appear that customers are more than happy to abandon on-board meals and complimentary drinks in favour of cheaper fares and their own sandwiches. Increasingly, bargain hunters are leaving it until the last minute to book holidays, making lastminute.com the most popular travel web site in the UK. In spite of these trends however, Thomson argues that in the long run holidaymakers will favour quality over price.

Questions

1. How can Thomson encourage its customers to buy their holidays early, thus protecting themselves from the last-minute bargain hunters? Suggestions that do not involve discounts would be welcome, given Thomson's strategy of quality over price.

2. What advice would you give Thomson on how to justify higher prices to customers?

3. Market segmentation sometimes helps with pricing strategy aimed at maximising income (differential pricing). How might this work for Thomson?

Sources

McLuhan, R. (1999) 'Thomson ads go for service', *Marketing,* 6 January, p21.
Murphy, D. (2000) 'Web travel takes off', *Marketing,* 19 October, p43.

SUMMARY OF KEY POINTS

- Pricing decisions need to take into account the total effect of the marketing mix.

- Strategies aimed at maximising income include price skimming, premium pricing, differential pricing and auction.

- Strategies aimed at maximising volume include penetration pricing and discounting. Penetration pricing is only advisable in certain circumstances (expanding market, well-resourced organisation).

- Costs (fixed and variable) can be used to calculate break-even points at various prices as a guide to price setting.

- Customers are the most important factor in pricing for marketers. The price elasticity of demand of a product is a measure of how well demand stands up to increases (or decreases) in price.

- Competitors also influence pricing decisions, especially in markets where there is little to choose between rival products apart from price.

Glossary of terms

auction: a public sale in which goods are sold to the highest bidder.

break-even analysis: calculating the point at which goods sold at a certain price will equal in value the cost of their manufacture.

cost-plus pricing: setting prices with reference to the cost of manufacture, adding a margin for profit.

differential pricing: charging different prices for the same goods or services to different market segments.

elastic demand: when levels of demand for a product or service rise or fall significantly if their prices are lowered or raised.

fixed costs: overheads which do not change with the quantity of something produced (also known as indirect costs).

inelastic demand: when levels of demand for a product or service remain fairly stable regardless of their price.

marginal cost: the cost of producing an additional unit of a product, when that product is already being produced.

premium pricing: using price to enhance perceptions of quality or luxury.

price elasticity of demand: a measure of how well demand for goods or services stands up in the face of price changes (also known as price sensitivity).

price penetration: pricing at a level which maximises volume rather than profit.

price skimming: pricing at a level which maximises profit rather than volume.

variable costs: costs which increase as extra quantities of something are produced (also known as direct costs).

Self-test multiple-choice questions

1. **In periods of high consumer demand, prices have a tendency to:**
   a) Go up.
   b) Go down.
   c) Stabilise.
   d) Remain constant.

2. **The strategy of charging a clearly defined group of customers a high price for a new product is known as:**
   a) Price elasticity.
   b) Price skimming.
   c) Penetration pricing.
   d) Auction.

3. **Which of the following costs would you normally classify as fixed (or indirect) costs?**
   a) Ingredients.
   b) Raw material.
   c) Packaging.
   d) Labour.

4. The break-even point is:
   a) Where demand meets supply in the market.
   b) Where sales revenue matches total costs.
   c) Where sales revenue matches fixed costs.
   d) Where the product is evenly distributed amongst market segments.

5. Terrikin Fruit Bars increased in price to 35p from 30p six months ago because of rising ingredient costs. The Board of Directors have noticed a 12% drop in sales year on year in the corresponding period since the price increase. Which of the following is true?
   a) The elasticity of demand is 0.72, demonstrating a relatively inelastic demand.
   b) The elasticity of demand is 0.72, demonstrating a relatively elastic demand.
   c) The elasticity of demand is 1.39 demonstrating a relatively inelastic demand.
   d) The elasticity of demand is 1.39 demonstrating a relatively elastic demand.

Something to think about...

1. What pricing options are open to a manufacturer launching a new product in one of the following markets? Office stationery, confectionery (the kind you buy for yourself), petrol, furniture, paint.

2. Are there any circumstances (thinking about your own experience as a buyer) where price discounting might not encourage you to buy more?

3. Which of the following are fixed costs and which are variable? Lighting, ingredients, labour, rent.

4. Discuss the view that markets with falling prices are in nobody's interest, including that of consumers.

5. What are the advantages of online auctions to buyers and sellers, and to the Internet companies (like Yahoo!) who host them?

Session 9

Place – making products and services available to customers

This Session looks at the issue of availability. No matter how good the product, how competitive the price and compelling the advertising, if we can't actually find the item all our marketing effort will be wasted. Distribution can make all the difference between marketing success and failure, and is an area that is constantly changing.

LEARNING OUTCOMES

At the end of this Session you should be able to:

- Distinguish between the major types of channel intermediary and explain their basic function.

- Outline the contribution made by distribution to customer value.

- Comment on reasons for marketers' choice of distribution strategy.

- Differentiate between selective, intensive and exclusive distribution, with examples.

- Discuss the role of e-commerce in distribution.

- Describe the basic processes of physical distribution.

STUDY TEXT

Marketing channels

Distribution is the choice and management of ways of making goods or services available to the maximum number of relevant customers at the minimum cost. It is one of the most important parts of marketing, but is the one we tend to take for granted. Perhaps this is because the more effective a distribution system is, the less noticeable it is to the consumer. Coca-Cola prides itself on a distribution strategy which puts its products "within an arm's reach of desire", an ideal of effortless availability to any customer at any place at any time.

Goods and services are made available to consumers through the operation of marketing channels. A marketing channel is a linked chain of individuals or organisations that connects producers to their final customers. The individuals or organisations that make up the chain are called intermediaries. This word literally means ways between buyers and sellers. There are two main types of intermediaries: merchants and functional intermediaries.

Merchants actually pay for and own the goods that are on their way to the final customer. This is known as taking title to the goods. In doing so they risk their own money by stocking the goods, just as manufacturers risk money by producing them in the first place. Merchants make money on the profit margins of their sales.

Functional intermediaries on the other hand, do not own the goods that pass through them. Rather than taking title, they help the actual owners find customers for their goods. Examples of such intermediaries are transport and distribution companies and agents. Functional intermediaries make money either on commission (whereby they keep an agreed percentage of the selling price of the goods) or a fee paid by the client, or even a mixture of both.

Functions of agents, merchants, wholesalers and retailers

Distribution channels earn their keep by making life easier for the final customer. Some of the ways in which they do this are by:

- Breaking down bulk (so customers can buy things in appropriate portions or sizes).

- Bringing together a convenient selection of goods from different suppliers (so customers have a choice, and can make a number of purchases at the same time).

- Providing storage and transportation (so customers don't have to build up their own stocks or spend ages travelling to and from suppliers).

- Giving advice and information (so customers can be confident they are making purchases which will deliver the benefits they are looking for).

Within this general process of creating convenience for the customer, different channel members have different functions. Figure 9.1 illustrates a variety of distribution channels of different lengths. Each contains a different selection of channel members whose precise functions we will examine in a moment. In marketing terminology the length of a distribution channel has little to do with geographical distance. It means instead the number of channel members involved. So, a company manufacturing engineering components in West Yorkshire, UK, but exporting them directly to a customer in Singapore, is using a very short distribution channel. On the other hand, in Japan, a country whose geography is relatively compact, distribution channels are notoriously long in many market sectors, involving a bewildering number of intermediaries.

Figure 9.1

Channel dimensions

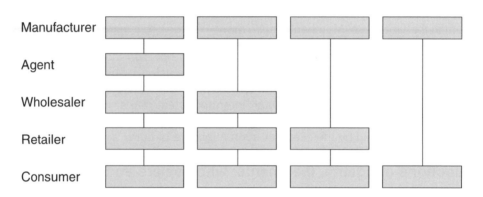

The longest channel here features manufacturer, agent, wholesaler, retailer and consumer. Their different functions are as follows:

An **agent** is a functional intermediary who represents a manufacturer (the client) in a particular market and arranges various marketing services (including advertising) at a price. Agents are common in international markets where clients cannot afford to maintain a direct presence. Using an agent gives a client access to specialist knowledge and contacts which otherwise might take years to build up. However, because agents work for a number of different clients, the relationship needs constant attention and review.

A **wholesaler** buys goods, either direct from a manufacturer or from an agent, and resells them to retailers (the next stage in most distribution channels before the consumer). Often wholesalers specialise in particular sorts of merchandise. Traditional wholesalers offer credit terms to their regular customers, and can also deliver direct to retailers. There is also a type of wholesaler called a Cash and Carry, which does not offer credit (hence the "cash" in the title). Such wholesalers do not offer delivery facilities, so their customers have to carry their purchases away themselves.

The **retailer** is the last stage in the chain before the goods reach the final consumer. Presentation and customer service are of great importance, in order to offer shoppers an experience they will want to return to. Some retailers specialise in particular sorts of merchandise (e.g. electrical goods, books or shoes) but there has been a trend towards the blurring of boundaries, as large food retailing chains seek new market sectors to expand into. Some retailers are so large that they have their own networks of depots and warehouses to which manufacturers deliver direct. This kind of distribution channel is also illustrated in Figure 9.1.

Wholesalers and retailers are merchants rather than functional intermediaries. The difference between a merchant and a functional intermediary is an important one in practical terms. Because they own the goods, merchants have far more control over the marketing of their merchandise. Agents, by contrast, have to follow the client's instructions. For example, an agent cannot make the final decision about the selling price of the goods being handled – whereas a merchant can. Sometimes this leads to clashes between merchant intermediaries and manufacturers, as the latter object to price cuts that they see as cheapening the image of their products.

Activity 9.1 On a role?

Distribution channels involve people dealing with other people. This exercise invites you to explore a difficult distribution situation through role play. Role playing is a way of learning by putting yourself imaginatively into a dramatic situation and exploring the motivations of those involved. It works best in a group – especially if any of your fellow students are good at drama! Get three people to study the roles of Mandy, Holly and Rita below and act out a three-minute drama based on what they might say to one another. Then discuss the issues raised in the class as a whole. If you are studying independently, try to imagine how the three characters might resolve their differences, and make some notes. Here is the scenario:

The Copgrove Chocolate company has just launched a new product called the Copbana – a luxurious chocolate bar, filled with banana mousse, over a layer of chewy caramel. As market research predicted, the bar is very popular as a self-indulgent treat, and is selling strongly in spite of its 60p price tag (which makes it considerably more expensive than the average chocolate bar). However, a hiccup has emerged with the innovative manufacturing process for the banana mousse and, as a result, initial production has been halved. In the mean time, demand for the new bars is outstripping supply to the point that the

---

company's sales force is having a tough time pacifying wholesalers and large retailers who are frustrated at losing potential sales because there is not enough stock to go round.

- Mandy Manufacturer: a new sales representative for Copgrove. You have 2,000 cases of Copbana this month, and the promise of 7,000 next month. Already you have orders for over 10,000 cases this month and 10,000 next month. You know you have only a fifth of what you need this month to keep the wholesalers and retailers in your area happy, and they still won't be pleased next month. Two customers in particular are on your mind as you prepare for a meeting: Holly Wholesaler and Rita Retailer.

- Holly Wholesaler: you run a medium-sized wholesale outlet that has increased its business with Copgrove by 20% in the last year. You are really counting on getting your full order of 1,000 cases of Copbana this month, as you have a promotion arranged and it's in your newsletter to retail customers.

- Rita Retailer: you are the confectionery purchasing manager of a regional chain, commanding 15% of the available grocery market. Copgrove is just one of the manufacturers you deal with, and you will not be best pleased with them if they cannot deliver the 8,000 cases you want this month.

Role play a meeting between Mandy and at least one of the others (perhaps face-to-face with Holly, but interrupted by a call on Mandy's mobile from an irate Rita). How can Mandy deal with the customers in a way which makes sense? Where there is insufficient information in this case, please specify the assumptions you are making.

Channel choice

The length and type of distribution channel selected varies according to a wide range of factors. It is common for manufacturers to use more than one kind of distribution channel as they target different market segments. In fact, a company could use all four of the channels illustrated in Figure 9.1 simultaneously. Take the example of a book publisher. It might try to open up a new market abroad by going through an agent, who can supply wholesalers and retailers in the new market, check that the books are displayed correctly and offer promotional support to get into new outlets. It might also deal with a number of book wholesalers in its domestic market, who then sell on to small bookshops who are not part of a major chain. At the same time, it might deal direct with the major bookselling chains, without going through a wholesaler. Finally, it might offer a mail order service, perhaps based on its web site, to individual customers direct.

We can summarise the effects of channel choice into three main varieties of distribution, as seen from the customer's point of view: intensive, selective and exclusive distribution.

Intensive distribution is where a manufacturer makes a product available through all the outlets prepared to stock it. Batteries or confectionery are good examples of intensively distributed products. They take up little space on a shelf or counter, are relatively high value (expensive) for their size, and therefore offer a good profit margin. They also require very little expertise to sell. As a result they are an attractive proposition to retailers of any sort – and can be found in garages, newsagents, grocers and chemists. Most importantly, they are frequently purchased by a wide range of customers, so a scatter-gun approach to distribution is highly appropriate.

Selective distribution is where a manufacturer makes a product available through a limited number of outlets. Electrical appliances, such as televisions or vacuum cleaners, are examples of selectively distributed products. They are relatively complicated to sell (often involving guarantees and instructions) and are purchased fairly infrequently by a defined range of customers. They tend to be sold in specialist shops – in this case electrical retailers. Customers know where to look for such goods, and tend to spend more time and money on their purchases than on goods bought more frequently.

Exclusive distribution is a more extreme form of selective distribution. Here the very restricted number of outlets through which a manufacturer offers a product is one of the benefits to the customer. This kind of distribution is often associated with luxury items such as designer label clothes or sports cars. However, it is not restricted to expensive goods. Certain sorts of toiletries are only available in outlets like Body Shop or Lush. Selling exclusively distributed goods often requires a high level of expertise and customer service, and manufacturers provide their nominated outlets with training and merchandising guidelines. Customers, most of them in niche markets, are happy to trade-off the inconvenience of seeking out exclusively distributed products for the prestige of owning and using them.

Activity 9.2 Channel vision

Prepare a diagram to illustrate either your own organisation's distribution channel(s) (remember it may have more than one), or one of the following:

a) An engineering firm in West Yorkshire, UK, exports tractor parts to European farmers, via an agent in France, who deals with retailers in France, Germany and Spain.

b) A confectionery manufacturer supplies a number of wholesalers who deal with smaller newsagents and corner shops.

E-commerce and distribution

Because distribution is such an important part of the marketing mix, it pays to keep an eye on changes. In particular, new technology has equipped marketers with plenty of opportunities to increase customer satisfaction, and their profits, in the area of distribution over the last twenty years. Many of these improvements have been thanks to the use of Information and Communication Technology (ICT). Universal bar-coding on packaging has allowed retailers to use information from Electronic Point of Sale (EPOS) scanning systems to check which lines are selling fastest in order to restock immediately. More recently they have been able to combine this information with data from individual customers' loyalty cards, which are swiped at the time of each purchase, to get a better sense of their customers as individuals.

Perhaps the single most exciting development in the area of technology and distribution recently has been the introduction of e-commerce. The rapid adoption of the Internet into many people's homes has opened up a powerful new channel connecting buyers and sellers.

E-commerce is trading activity that takes place on the Internet, usually through a buyer visiting a seller's web site and completing a transaction there. So far the vast majority of such transactions have taken place between businesses (business-to-business, or b2b as it is known). But the importance of business-to-consumer (b2c) e-commerce is growing. Alongside this trend, the Internet is playing an ever increasing part in consumers' purchasing behaviour in general. While in the year 2000 only 3% of all the cars sold in the U.S. were sold via e-commerce, 40% of all

U.S. car sales involved the Internet at some stage (as a source of information or price guide).

For buyers, the Internet offers instant price comparisons and a vast choice of products and suppliers. It also allows buyers to band together with others to negotiate bulk discounts, through a practice known as customer aggregation. For suppliers, the Internet offers a direct path to customers. It allows them to tailor their offer to the individual customer far more economically than through traditional channels.

In fact, the growth of e-commerce has threatened traditional distribution intermediaries with a process known as **disintermediation.** In other words they may be rendered redundant. Thinking back to our earlier list of functions carried out by distribution channels, it is clear that the Internet offers many of the benefits listed – breaking down bulk, bringing together a convenient selection in one place, giving advice and information. However, it is not so good at storage and transportation. Early Internet shoppers who decided to rely on e-commerce for Christmas 1999 were dismayed when their purchases arrived too late for the festive season because of stock problems and delivery hiccups.

The way ahead for b2c e-commerce is to combine the speed and convenience of ordering from a web site with the reassurance of a real-life shop outlet. This pattern of trading, known as **"clicks'n'bricks"** or **"clicks and mortar",** has proved successful for the UK retailer Tesco, whose Internet shopping service, Tesco Direct, is now the world's largest Internet grocer. Even e-commerce operations that started out solely on the Internet have now opened high-street outlets – if only to give dissatisfied customers somewhere to return faulty goods!

Instead of putting existing distribution intermediaries completely out of business, e-commerce has found new uses for them in providing the essential physical presence they lack. There is also an argument that suggests the growth of e-commerce will require new intermediaries, providing services such as secure credit card number facilities, or protecting the anonymity of web shoppers from suppliers. These new services, peculiar to the world of e-commerce, will be supplied by infomediaries; companies dedicated to facilitating e-commerce transactions.

Activity 9.3 Virtual retailing

Many of the doubts about the viability of consumer e-commerce have been based on the differences between shopping experiences in a physical location and on a computer.

Browse one of the retail sites to be found at http://www.kelkoo.co.uk, and compile a list of ways in which it tries to reproduce (or improve upon) the physical shopping experience, particularly in the following areas:

- Bringing together a selection of goods and services.
- Corporate identity (the image of the site, compared with the image of a shop).
- Fun and social interaction.
- Helping customers find what they are looking for.
- Providing impulse purchase opportunities.
- Providing advice and information (e.g. descriptions and displays).

Physical distribution

An essential part of satisfying customers is to get goods to them in the right condition and at a convenient time. This is where **physical distribution,** the process of moving products from suppliers to users, comes in. This process can be broken into five stages in order to aid analysis and assist marketers in identifying potential improvements. These are order processing, materials handling, warehousing, inventory management and transport.

Order processing is the beginning of the chain of events that follows the placing of an order with a supplier. The more efficiently and accurately an order can be dealt with, the greater the satisfaction the final customer will enjoy. This is because an efficient order processing system will minimise any possible delays or mistakes. If the goods requested are not available, prompt notification of the fact will allow an alternative to be proposed, or at least avoid any unpleasant surprises for the customer. In the case of consumer shopping, order processing often goes no further than a retailer presenting products for self-selection in a way which makes sense to customers, and helps them choose goods, like groceries or clothing, in the most convenient way. As with business-to-business transactions however, this may prove a decisive factor in winning and keeping customers.

Materials handling covers all the details of moving and storing goods in an appropriate way. Clearly, the sort of treatment they require depends on the kind of goods involved. Bulky or dangerous items need conditions that guarantee security and safety. Food products and other perishable goods tend to require chilled storage and rapid transfer to the user. Materials handling has a direct impact on quality and convenience, and decisions here can have a profound effect on other aspects of physical distribution and, consequently, on customer loyalty.

Warehousing is closely connected to materials handling, but looks at the wider issues of where to site warehouses and depots, as well as the conditions created inside them. Computerisation and economies of scale have been the major driving forces in this area of physical distribution over the last two decades. The size of warehouses has been increasing whilst the number of people employed in them has decreased, in an ongoing search for efficiency. This can mean greater convenience as well as lower prices for customers, again contributing to an edge over competitors.

Inventory control is the fine art of keeping enough stock available at any one time to cover unexpected surges in demand, but not so much as to tie up too much of the company's money. Again, computerisation has been an important influence. By modelling patterns of demand, companies can minimise the amount of unnecessary stock. This liberates money to be used better elsewhere in the business, as well as saving on storage costs. A good example of inventory control is the McDonald's system, which uses a computer model to predict demand in individual branches, minute by minute, in order to prevent cooked burgers from standing too long on the shelf and thus losing flavour.

Transport is another part of the process that is intimately connected to materials handling. Wisely chosen transport arrangements can add significantly to a customer's convenience, in terms of getting a product to the right place at the right time. The nature of the product itself is an important consideration. The decision as to what kind of transport to use (most companies use a combination of road, rail, water and air) and whether to buy in the services of a functional intermediary or do it direct is an important one. Some companies have their own fleet of vehicles which, appropriately liveried, can be a useful source of free advertising as they roll up and down the nation's roads.

Activity 9.4 Service distribution

Most of the ideas in this Session refer to distribution of physical goods. Yet services such as banking, energy and communications are actually worth more in many Western economies. Taking a service industry with which you are familiar (perhaps insurance or transport), can you identify processes that match the following aspects of physical distribution management?

- Order processing.

- Materials handling.

- Warehousing.

- Inventory management.

- Transport.

Don't worry if you cannot get exact equivalents of each – the purpose of this exercise is to get you to think creatively rather than solve a puzzle. Applying lessons from physical goods to service industries can lead to some original insights. The marketers who launched GO, one of the first cut-price airlines, are said to have been inspired by the way that Swatch pioneered a cheap, but high-quality version of a prestige product – the Swiss watch.

Then read Hill and O'Sullivan (2004) *Foundation Marketing* (3rd Edition) FT/Prentice Hall, pages 265-295 and 322-326 and self-check questions 3, 7, 13 and 15 for Chapter 10.

Activity 9.5 How much is enough?

A regular problem for warehouse managers is the question of how often they should reorder stock from a supplier, and in what quantity. The cost of the stock itself ties up money of course, but it also costs money to place the order (administrative work, communication, travel, etc.) and to look after the stock (insurance, rental, security, the effects of inflation, etc.). Get too little and you end up spending more than you have to on ordering costs, because you are placing orders too often. Get too much and you face spiralling costs from having to look after it. How much then is enough?

The solution to this question is computerised nowadays, but the principles on which the computer programmes work are based on a simple mathematical formula.

Optimum economic order quantity = $\sqrt{((2 \times \text{cost of ordering} \times D)/\text{handling cost})}$

The formula needs you to know the following values:

- The total stock demanded by customers from the warehouse in a typical year (here called D for demand).
- The cost of ordering (rather than the cost of the goods themselves).
- The average cost of looking after one unit of stock per year (handling cost).

Let's say you sell 300 specialist components a year from your warehouse, making D 300. Suppose too that because of the way your company works, the cost of making an order, whatever its size, is estimated at £40, to cover administration etc. Finally, let's say that your accountants have worked out the average cost of storing one of these components for a year is £6. The formula works out as follows:

Optimum economic order quantity = $\sqrt{((2 \times 40 \times 300)/6)}$
= $\sqrt{(24000)/6}$
= $\sqrt{(4000)}$
= 63.25

Rounding this to 63 gives us the most advantageous balance between the costs of ordering and the cost of looking after the stock. So we would be looking at making approximately five orders a year to bring us to the required level of 300 units to cover demand.

Now try the calculation yourself using the following data:

a) Demand (D) = 600, Ordering cost (fixed) = £30, Handling cost = £8.
b) Demand (D) = 1500, Ordering cost (fixed) = £20, Handling cost = £4.
c) Demand (D) = 3000, Ordering cost (fixed) = £40, Handling cost = £2.

This rather abstract way of thinking about order quantities is useful up to a point, but what other factors might a warehouse manager bear in mind when deciding how much and how often to order?

Activity 9.6

CASE STUDY: Grocer-e shopping hits a snag

One of the most promising dotcoms to have gone belly-up in recent years is Webvan, an Internet-based firm that had its eye on the American grocery market. At its launch in 1999, it promised Internet shoppers in America a complete grocery service. Webvan's plans included building a $1 billion network of warehouses in America, before taking its business idea abroad and conquering the rest of the web-wide world.

Early investors were impressed by the company's flagship 330,000 square foot warehouse, or distribution centre, at Oakland, in the cheaper part of San Francisco Bay. The warehouse had three sections, colour-coded to reflect storage temperature. Yellow denoted standard groceries like tinned vegetables or pasta. The green zone was for chilled foods – for example, dairy products. Blue, as you might expect, was the coldest zone – offering temperatures of minus 20 degrees for frozen goods. Robotic "mechpods" (giant, insect-like machines) shifted heavier groceries around. Stock levels in each of the zones were monitored by computer, and reordering done as necessary using Internet links with suppliers.

In its heyday 2,000 orders were processed each day by a staff of about 150 packers. Each order involved an average of 10 shopping baskets, or "totes", colour coded to reflect the zone from which the orders were picked. As totes travelled around the warehouse on a conveyor belt, a light display let each packer know what merchandise was required. The warehouse's layout meant no packer needed to move more than 20 feet to reach the relevant groceries in his or her section.

Completed orders were then transferred from this central location to a number of smaller delivery centres dotted around it in the local area. This kind of "hub and spokes" system is a popular model in traditional physical distribution management. The orders then travelled on the company's distinctive vans to reach customers in their homes within pre-booked half-hour slots. In the first two years of operation the success rate in hitting these slots ran at 98%.

As well as convenience, Webvan customers benefited from product freshness (with meat, fish and vegetables directly sourced from suppliers) and prices running at about 5% less than those found in traditional outlets. In order to get customers to try the service, free delivery was offered on all orders during the launch period, before being restricted to orders above $50.

Webvan's figurehead, Mr George Shaheen, came from a background of high-flying management consultancy. Investors were impressed by his credentials, but it looks as if he was better at the theory of marketing than the practice. Mounting costs led to his resignation in April 2001, three months before the company filed for bankruptcy, after the kind of cash flow crisis that has scuppered many a promising e-business.

Even in its more buoyant days, Webvan's critics had pointed out that the operation was an expensive one. Building a network of state-of-the-art warehouses does not come cheap, and the van service represented a substantial cost. In defence Shaheen pointed out that his warehouses required almost a third less staff than supermarkets of a similar size, and that his property costs were also a fraction of those of his supermarket rivals, who needed to be sited in popular areas. Webvan, on the other hand, was free to choose the cheapest sites.

Questions

1. Describe the five elements of physical distribution, illustrating them from the Webvan example.

2. Imagine you are trying to relaunch Webvan, having found a solution to the costs problem. How would you answer a critic who says that Webvan will never really catch on, because people like to be able to touch and feel products like fruit and vegetables before they buy them?

3. Some industry commentators claim that Internet grocers will never take more than a small share of the available market. Please give your reasons for either agreeing or disagreeing with this view.

Source

Economist (2000) 'Saturday morning syndrome', Survey: E-Commerce, 26th February, p26.
Economist (2001) 'Big is beautiful again', 21st July, pp65-6.

SUMMARY OF KEY POINTS

- Marketing channels connect producers to consumers through a network of organisations and individuals called channel members or intermediaries.

- Merchant intermediaries actually buy and sell goods. Functional intermediaries facilitate such transactions.

- Basic distribution strategies include: intensive distribution (wide availability), selective distribution (specific types of outlet) and exclusive distribution (a very limited number of outlets).

- ICT has driven many recent developments in distribution, the Internet in particular.

- Physical distribution is the process of physically moving goods from suppliers to users. It involves order processing, materials handling, warehousing, inventory management and transport. Improvements in each of these areas can have a direct effect on increasing the satisfaction of the final customer.

Glossary of terms

agents: channel members who arrange transactions, but do not themselves buy the products with which they deal.

b2b, b2c: business-to-business, business-to-consumer, respectively – terms used to describe e-commerce transactions.

channel: a grouping of individuals or institutions who create links between buyers and sellers.

channel conflict: clashes of interest between distribution intermediaries, either horizontal (between intermediaries at the same stage in two separate channels) or vertical (between successive intermediaries in the same channel).

clicks'n'bricks, clicks and mortar: a model of e-commerce that combines a presence on the web with physical retail outlets.

disintermediation: the replacement of traditional distribution channels by the use of the Internet.

e-commerce: trading activity which takes place on the Internet, usually through a buyer visiting a seller's web site and completing a transaction there.

exclusive distribution: appointing a select group of distributors to sell a product.

infomediary: an intermediary offering services which facilitate e-commerce.

intensive distribution: selling goods through all the intermediaries willing to distribute them.

intermediaries: organisations or individuals who facilitates the transfer of goods or services from producers to consumers (also known as distributors).

inventory: the amount and variety of stock carried by a business.

functional intermediaries: channel members who facilitate exchanges without actually owning the goods they handle.

merchants: channel members who buy and re-sell the industrial products with which they deal.

physical distribution: the process of moving products from suppliers to users.

retailers: channel members who buy consumer goods and re-sell them to consumers.

selective distribution: selling goods through some but not all of the available distributors.

wholesalers: channel members who buy consumer goods and re-sell them to retailers.

Self-test multiple-choice questions

1. **A distribution strategy that ensures availability of a product through all the outlets willing to stock it is known as:**
   a) Intensive distribution.
   b) Extensive distribution.
   c) Exclusive distribution.
   d) Inclusive distribution.

2. **The role of distribution intermediaries in allowing customers to buy products in convenient quantities is known as:**
   a) Storage.
   b) Breaking down bulk.
   c) Transport.
   d) Giving advice.

3. **In marketing terminology, the length of a distribution channel is proportional to which one of the following?**
   a) The geographical distance between the supplier and the final customer.
   b) The length of time it takes for a product to pass through the channel.
   c) The number of channel members.
   d) The mode of transport used.

4. **Which one of the following is a merchant intermediary rather than a functional intermediary?**
   a) Retailer.
   b) Agent.
   c) Road haulier.
   d) Shipping company.

5. **The retailer is the last link in the distribution chain before...**
   a) The wholesaler.
   b) The agent.
   c) The consumer.
   d) The manufacturer.

Something to think about...

1. What factors would you take into account when deciding where to open a new branch of Marks & Spencer?

2. Drawing on your own experience as a customer, list the advantages and disadvantages of: telephone banking, Internet bookshops, drive-thru McDonald's.

3. How do distribution intermediaries create customer convenience in the following markets: food retailing, dry-cleaning, live sporting events, fitness and health?

4. Discuss the differences between making a film available on DVD (to rent or to buy) and releasing it in cinemas, from the point of view of producer, retailer and consumer.

5. What are the advantages and disadvantages of using an agent rather than a merchant intermediary?

Session 10

Promotion – getting the message across

This Session deals with promotion – the part of the marketing mix that communicates the benefits of a product to customers. For many people it is the first thing they think of when marketing is mentioned, although there is much more to marketing than just a clever advertisement or an original public relations stunt. However, promotion is becoming more and more important to marketing activity, as marketers fight to make themselves heard in an increasingly noisy environment.

LEARNING OUTCOMES

At the end of this Session you should be able to:

- Outline and illustrate a simple communication model (AIDA).

- Distinguish between "push" and "pull" communication strategies.

- Describe the main strengths and weaknesses of a range of common promotional methods.

- Demonstrate an understanding of common terms used in connection with marketing communications using electronic media.

STUDY TEXT

AIDA model of marketing communication

Models are useful in helping us understand how things work and how we can improve on them. When a theatre designer is developing a set design, he or she will build an accurate scale model of the set. Amongst other things, the model helps to work out how much the set will cost and how it will function. Clearly, the set model is not the real thing – it is a useful representation.

In the same way marketing uses models. You may already be familiar with models of how consumers make decisions, or how products go through a life cycle from earlier Sessions. Now we will look at another model – a representation of how communication works. It can be extremely useful in designing and managing promotional activity. This model is known as AIDA – an acronym (a word made up of the initials of other words). AIDA stands for:

Attention
Interest
Desire
Action

It describes the sequence of events that occurs in an effective act of promotional communication.

AIDA is a marketing classic, dating from America in the early 1900s. But it is still very useful for thinking about how promotion works in marketing. Communication in general, and promotion in particular, is far more complex than the model. But models are judged by their usefulness rather than their truth to life.

AIDA suggests that effective advertising takes customers through four stages. First their **attention** is attracted by a striking or original idea or image. At this point they may not even understand what is going on – they are just stopped in their tracks by a compelling headline in a press ad, or an image jumping out of a TV commercial or poster. There are so many other calls on our attention that being noticed is quite a tall order for an advertisement. This stage, sometimes referred to as "cut-through" by advertisers, is therefore vitally important if any effective communication is to take place.

The second phase is **interest.** Once gained, attention must be held in order to get a message across. Interest is the key to this. In other words the communication must be relevant enough to the target audience to make them feel like stopping and taking notice. In a TV advert or poster, interest is often maintained by using a celebrity or an image meaningful to the target audience. In a press ad, the interest is often created by what is said early on – an intriguing fact, or a teasing question. The focus of interest clearly needs to be the product and what it can do for the customer.

Desire should follow interest. The customer moves from a general interest in what is being said, to a particular realisation of how this product will satisfy a specific need. Desire is often aided by a product demonstration, dramatising how the customer can benefit from its purchase. This should establish the need for the product in the customer's mind. TV advertising is particularly good at dramatising the use of a product. In a sales encounter, this stage of the process often takes the shape of the customer trying out the product. Test-driving a car is a good example. As you experience the car yourself, you have a much more vivid sense of whether you desire it.

Action ends the process. The action aimed at is usually purchase, but it might be that an interim action is the objective (such as applying for a membership pack, or even changing one's attitude to an issue or cause). Action in many press adverts boils down to cutting out a reply coupon and mailing it with an order, or perhaps ringing a credit card hotline or visiting a web site. Action in the context of a TV commercial is usually delayed until a purchase opportunity arises (although a significant number of TV commercials have a telephone number for instant responses).

Activity 10.1 Colourful advertising

Equip yourself with four different colour pens or highlighters. Find a full-page press advert in a newspaper or magazine. Underline (or highlight) the different elements of the advertisement in the four different colours, e.g.

Attention: Red.
Interest: Blue.
Desire: Green.
Action: Black.

If possible, compare your findings with another student's work, and see if you agree about which elements of the advert correspond to which aspects of the ad.

Push and Pull strategies

Marketing terminology makes a distinction between push and pull strategies in promotion. A **push** strategy concentrates on channel intermediaries. The manufacturer's sales force offer discounts and bonuses as incentives to wholesalers and retailers to stock and display products. The products are thus pushed towards the customer, who becomes aware of them mainly through point-of-sale displays or in-store demonstrations. This form of promotion is important for many goods like washing machines or vacuum cleaners, where wide distribution is essential in an extremely competitive market. Concentrating the marketing effort on intermediaries, often known as trade marketing, helps gain vital access to the end customer.

Pull promotion, on the other hand, ignores the distribution channel and goes straight for the final user. By arousing the interest and desire of the customer, who will then act by asking for it, pull promotion aims to create a demand for the product. This will "pull" it through the channel of distribution. Retailers and wholesalers will be forced to stock the product if enough people ask for it. Advertising, editorial public relations and consumer sales promotion are the main weapons here. Whilst this is more common with consumer goods and services, pull promotion is sometimes used by companies more immediately associated with industrial products. A computer chip manufacturer, Intel, used television and poster advertising in the UK to heighten consumer's awareness of its brand name. By creating the expectation amongst users that Intel chips should be inside their computers, Intel has made their component more attractive to computer hardware manufacturers.

Although push and pull strategies are different, they are also complementary. Most, if not all, organisations use a combination of the two approaches in order to compete effectively.

Uses, advantages and limitations of common promotional techniques

There are a number of techniques that can be used to communicate the benefits of your product to customers in a way that may win their business or may keep them buying. Each has its own strengths and weaknesses in different situations. In this section we will briefly review advertising, editorial Public Relations (PR), sales promotion and personal selling.

Advertising is the use of paid-for media to inform and/or influence existing or potential customers. It is perhaps the first promotional technique that comes to mind, because of our familiarity as readers, listeners and viewers with the barrage of adverts that compete for our attention every day. This quality of being all around us is one of advertising's strengths. It is very difficult to avoid. But this is also the basis of its weakness. There is simply so much of it that it is difficult for advertisers to make an impact without spending a great deal of money. However, advertising remains one of the most successful ways of creating and sustaining a brand – an essential concept in profitable marketing (see Session 7).

Traditionally, advertising is neither created nor bought directly by the organisations that pay for it. Instead they delegate this complicated job to advertising agencies – specialist companies who think up the ads, produce them, and place them where the target audience will see them. This involves buying space in newspapers, magazines, or poster sites, or time slots in cinemas, radio or television, for the best price they can negotiate, and then billing the manufacturer (the client) for the cost. In a sense agencies are therefore selling the services of media owners to their clients. In recognition of this, registered agencies receive commission from media owners on the media they buy. Such media expenditure is called **above the line,** to distinguish it from the many other sorts of promotional expenditure that are not commissionable (sales promotion, printed leaflets, press releases, etc.).

Activity 10.2 Campaign costs

Media rates (the prices which media owners charge for advertising) change throughout the year to reflect demand. Often these changes are expressed in industry information by what is known as indexing. Indexing involves emphasising the changes between one figure and another by expressing all the figures as percentages of some other unchanging value.

In this case, the value is the average monthly cost of advertising on television. You can see that advertising in January was 22% less expensive than average, whereas in May it was 10% more expensive than average.

Jan	Feb	Mar	Apr	May	Jun	Jul	Aug	Sep	Oct	Nov	Dec	Yr
78	90	95	105	110	110	102	90	110	110	115	100	100

a) If it cost £5.50 to reach 1,000 consumers using television in April, how much would it cost in August?

b) Can you re-profile the series of figures to start from January as 100, in order to emphasise the changes over the year more sharply?

Some advertising agencies specialise in creative work (making up and producing the advertising), others do nothing except buy media (getting impressive discounts because of the buying power they can wield), and there are others again who offer a full service. Some advertising agencies have even branched out into offering other forms of marketing communication besides advertising. This not only helps them to grow as a business, it also offers their clients a one-stop-shop, where they can organise and integrate their promotional activity across a number of techniques. This growing trend in centrally planned and executed promotion is called **integrated marketing communications.**

Advertising allows you to target your message closely to an audience because of the wide variety of media available. There is plenty of research available about what kind of people use which sort of media, even down to the kind of audiences individual TV shows attract! So, you can be reasonably certain about how many of your target market will have seen your advertising campaign. This concept is known as **coverage** – the proportion of the target market that the advertising has reached at least once. There is an associated idea of **frequency** – how many times, on average, each target customer will see an advert in a particular campaign. Because you are paying for it, you can repeat the message as often as you like. This is one of the big differences between advertising and editorial PR, where press releases will only be news on a particular day.

Public Relations (PR) is a wide field of activity that covers all the ways in which an organisation establishes and manages mutual understanding with its publics (the people who matter to it). Editorial PR, or **press relations,** is one way in which public relations can be put into practice. Rather than buying space in a publication, where it is clearly marked as advertising, **press relations** hitches a ride for your message in the news or features columns, by encouraging the media to report favourably on your product or organisation.

Because print and broadcast journalists are always on the lookout for news and ideas that will interest their audiences, they are receptive to what organisations can offer in the way of material. Clearly this must be sufficiently newsworthy to justify their consideration – journalists don't like the idea of being exploited to facilitate free advertising. So the key to successful press relations is to do some research into what works well in the media you are targeting, and couch your offering accordingly. Readers and viewers are the customers of the journalist. What benefits can your story, picture or media clip offer them?

Many press relations experts come from a journalistic background and are therefore good at spotting stories and couching them in attractive terms. The great strength of editorial PR as a technique is its credibility (which explains its importance to service industries like tourism or entertainment, where customers want reassurance before making a risky purchase). Because journalists are independent commentators, readers are more likely to believe what they say. On the other hand, using press relations means that an organisation hands over direct control of its message to a third party. It may be that the journalist gets it wrong, or represents the product or service in a rather unflattering way.

In spite of the potential for disaster, another strength of press relations is its cost-effectiveness. PR managers often judge their success by working out how much the media time or space occupied by their material would have cost to buy as advertising. However, this is a misleading comparison. Not only does press relations consume considerable amounts of time and resources, but advertising works in a different way. Having paid for it, the advertiser can count on its appearance and accuracy. By contrast, any press relations activity is entirely at the mercy of what else is making the news that day. It may be that a carefully planned story or picture never appears because a late-breaking story edges it out of the publication or programme. The true cost-effectiveness of editorial PR lies in its credibility, and the fact that it reaches audiences who are resistant to advertising.

Sales promotion aims to stimulate activity between customers and suppliers by increasing the speed or volume of a transaction. In simple terms, this means it gives customers a reason to buy something earlier, or more of it, than they would normally. It is a very flexible marketing communications technique that can be successfully applied either to the final consumer or to intermediaries in the distribution channel. It can thus be used for both pull and push promotion.

Sales promotions can take a wide variety of forms. The common element is to offer an incentive of some sort to stimulate purchase. Free gifts, competitions, discounts, free products, are all common techniques. As well as its flexibility, the main strengths of the technique are that it makes products stand out, by adding something extra, and that the effects on sales are immediately visible.

A corresponding weakness of sales promotion is, however, that it can appear gimmicky. Most promotions do not last longer than two or three months, and any increase in sales tend not to survive the promotion period. Indeed, there is research that suggests discount-based promotions rarely, if ever, pay for themselves through achieving lasting increases in sales. Defenders reply that the benefits of sales promotion include reviving interest in a product amongst distributors and customers, and that sales increases alone are not the best way to judge success. Furthermore, the increased use of integrated marketing communications means that sales promotions can be themed to work more effectively with long-term advertising, to develop brand image rather than confuse or cheapen it by short-term gimmicks.

Activity 10.3 Pocket-money profits

Advertising to children is a controversial topic because of the concerns about exploiting their vulnerability and encouraging anti-social pestering behaviour. The Internet, because of its interactive potential, has offered advertisers an exciting new medium to reach children, with the potential of offering them fun and entertainment as well as commercial messages. Compare and contrast two web sites from the following industries, focusing on how interesting and involving the material is, and how ethical their approach to communicating to younger audiences is.

a) Branded toys.
b) Breakfast cereals.
c) Confectionery.
d) Publishing (including comics).
e) Television programmes.

See if you can draw up a list of guidelines (aim for about 10 points) to encourage an ethical but effective approach to web content in this area.

Selling

All three of the marketing communication techniques we have looked at so far use large-scale media to communicate with large audiences. Selling, on the other hand, is on a smaller scale, a more personal affair. We can define it simply as interpersonal activity that facilitates the purchase of goods and services. Because it involves people it is very powerful, but also very expensive. Like any scarce resource, selling has to be accountable and used carefully.

Selling is the fundamental promotional technique used in business-to-business marketing. The number of buyers and sellers involved in such transactions is much smaller than in consumer marketing, and the average value of each transaction is much higher. Selling is therefore economical in this situation, whereas it would not be in consumer marketing. But while most consumers do not experience personal selling when buying products like groceries for example, salespeople deal with the wholesalers and retailers through whom the groceries find their way onto the shelves. However, selling does come into the consumers' direct experience in markets such as financial services, cars or computers. Here the need for information and advice, combined with the value of the purchase, justifies the expense of the technique.

Selling begins with prospecting. Rather like marketing research and market segmentation, this involves finding out who might be interested in your product and discovering more about them. No matter how good your offer, if it is irrelevant to the customer, or if you are talking to the wrong person, you will not make a sale. Having identified a likely prospect, the next stage is to make an approach. In business-to-business selling this involves setting up an appointment that gives you access to the decision maker.

The all-important presentation can now take place. This is the point at which you and the customer have a personal interaction. The AIDA model is useful in helping plan this encounter. Attention can be gained through appropriate dress and behaviour, a greeting, or even a smile. Interest can be maintained through asking questions aimed at getting a clearer idea of what the buyer's needs are. Once these are established in the salesperson's mind, desire should follow as he or she draws attention to precisely those aspects of the product which are best equipped to satisfy the buyer's particular needs. This responsiveness and interactivity is what gives personal selling its power as a marketing communication technique. Assuming an accurate diagnosis of needs, and a relevant account of the product's benefits, the action of purchase should complete the encounter.

Of course life is usually not that simple, and part of the training of a salesperson is to develop techniques that help control the situation, in order to guarantee consistency of customer service and encourage a positive outcome. One such technique is what is known as "closing" – helping the customer to come to a final commitment. Choices of any sort mean giving up some options – and sometimes customers can be reluctant to decide on a purchase there and then. However, because time is a scarce resource in selling (and in life!) part of the salesperson's job is to speed up the process by giving a positive opportunity for the decision. Simply asking for the order is one way of doing this, but such a request needs to be judged sensitively. More subtle ways include what is known as the "alternative close", where a choice of colour for example, is offered on the assumption that the customer has made up his or her mind to buy the product, but has not yet decided on the precise details. Such a tactic either results in a commitment there and then, or stimulates more information from the customer that can be used to place the product in a more attractive light as the negotiation continues.

The final stage of selling is follow-up. Many products include some kind of post-purchase relationship, such as training or servicing. But even where this does not exist as a requirement, keeping in touch with existing customers makes sense. Not only are they an essential source of continuing and new business, but they can often provide information valuable for accessing new prospects.

Activity 10.4 Extending AIDA

In this Session we have looked at how you can transfer the AIDA model from one form of marketing communication (advertising) to another (a sales encounter). Now try transferring the model to another situation again. Pick one of the following activities (whichever is most important to your own work environment). On one side of a piece of A4 paper map out the AIDA process through the four stages in order to make your performance clearer and more effective.

a) A telephone call.
b) A business letter.
c) A party invitation.
d) A conversation asking to borrow something.

Also read Hill and O'Sullivan (2004) *Foundation Marketing* (3rd Edition) FT/Prentice Hall, pages 299-305; Advertising 305-309, 312-315; Sales Promotion 349-358; PR 359-369; Internet 320-322 and self-check questions 2, 3, 6 and 14 (on pages 329-331).

Internet Promotion (web sites and Internet advertising)

Technology is one of the driving forces behind promotional opportunities. Print and broadcast technologies have provided marketers over the years with powerful means of communication. But media such as press, posters and television have addressed target markets impersonally, as a mass, and only carried messages one way. The Internet has now emerged as a promotional medium with enormous potential to communicate with each member of a large audience in a personalised way, and to facilitate immediate feedback (especially purchases) from customers.

Investors and marketing theorists have become very excited about this developing technology. Many declare that it has introduced a new way of marketing. There is some force to the argument. Businesses of any size can have a **home page** on the web, whether they are multinational corporations or sole traders. At a stroke their details are available to millions of potential customers worldwide. As we have seen in Session 9, the nature of trading on the Internet has threatened the rationale for a large number of companies involved in distribution. A less excited view of the Internet is that it is a bit like the telephone. As we get more and more used to the technology, the apparent differences between Internet marketing and traditional ways of serving customers will seem less and less significant.

The **Internet** is an international network of computers that are linked by telephone lines, or dedicated cables. In order to gain access to the network, you need to be connected to it by an **Internet Service Provider.** ISPs have huge computers called **servers,** because they serve up web pages to the rest of the network. Many ISPs also run **portals,** which act as a gateway for users, and guides them to other web pages of interest. Without a portal to guide you, the vastness of the **World Wide Web** can be daunting. Portals are an attractive location for advertising and sponsorship activity because of the potential traffic of users through them. Many portals are built around Internet **Search Engines;** special software that helps users find information by matching web pages to keyword searches, as described in Session 3's discussion on using the web as a source of information.

Many organisations use the power of web technology for internal communications. Their networks are called Intranets, to distinguish them from the Internet. An **Intranet** is not accessible to people outside a defined group of users, and its web pages contain documents, communication areas and official information pertinent to a particular organisation.

Each computer also has an individual address (called an **Internet Protocol (IP) number**), so that the computer files can find their way round. This is marvellous news for marketers trying to communicate with customers, because it means they can track which computers have visited their web pages, and store information on individual users' browsing and purchasing habits. By spotting which pages a particular visitor looked at longest, and by remembering what, if anything, they bought, marketers can make customised offerings the next time they visit the site. To help them do this, most web pages are designed to leave small identification files called **cookies** in the memory of the machines that visit them. This capability to adapt an offer to an individual on the basis of the needs he or she is revealing is much closer to selling than to traditional advertising. It is likely that the future of Internet advertising will become more like selling than the kind of brand-building advertising with which we are currently familiar.

Early Internet advertisers regarded it in much the same way as press advertising however. They bought space on popular sites in the form of banner advertisements, in the same way as they might buy part of a printed page. **Banner ads** are rectangular areas, usually at the top of web pages. When clicked on they take the user to the web page of the advertiser, like an active link. The initial results suggested gratifyingly high **click-through rates** (the percentage of visitors actually taking the link), but subsequent experience suggests that this was due to novelty. More recently it has emerged that Internet users are less interested in browsing (i.e. moving happily from one page to another to see what's out there) than in a purposeful use of the net. This being the case, they are irritated, rather than intrigued, by banner advertising. Click-through rates have plummeted, forcing advertisers to look at other possibilities. A more effective formula seems to be to include links to purchasing opportunities within editorial matter, so content about writers or musicians will have links embedded in the text to take the reader to a site like Amazon.com where the book or music can be bought.

Other bright advertising ideas on the Internet include **media-rich banners** (which are like mini web sites in their own right, but do not take you away from the site you are browsing), **pop-ups** (which are pages which pop up automatically among the pages you actually want to see) and the humble but effective **email.** Pop-ups are actually so irritating to web users as to be counter-productive in many cases. Email is easier to deal with, and you can take steps to avoid unwanted commercial email (called spam) by blocking your address from unwanted advertisers.

Three developments in the Internet as a marketing communications tool seem likely to gain momentum over the next few years. The first is that customers will become a lot more canny about the information they divulge about themselves to advertisers. Records about what you browsed and what you bought are not much use in themselves without information about what sort of a person you are. At the moment the only way in which Internet advertisers can access that kind of information is to buy it from consumers. Registering on some web sites carries with it a cash reward or a chance to win a prize, in exchange for the personal information you are asked to divulge.

The second development is a move away from advertising as we know it, to a form of co-operative selling known as an affiliate deal. Essentially this involves an advertiser joining forces with a successful web site, in order to offer a purchasing opportunity. Rather than paying for the exposure and hoping that sales will result, the advertiser agrees to share the sales revenue with the web site. Instead of being an advertising medium, this transforms the web site into a retail outlet.

The final development is that devices other than personal computers will be used to access the Internet. Indeed, some industry observers have predicted the demise of the computer as we know it, in favour of more portable and user-friendly devices. The rapid adoption of mobile telephones by consumers has spurred the development of **Wireless Application Protocol (WAP)** devices, which connect to the Internet through radio waves rather than cables. The ability to address individual customers with promotional messages on the move raises issues about privacy and ethics for marketers. Such promotion needs to be carefully targeted and carried out with permission so as not to irritate or alienate customers.

Activity 10.5 Ambient ambitions

Working in a small group devise a solution to the following problem. Ambient media is the name given to the various sorts of minor advertising media which do not quite fit into the main sectors of poster, press, and broadcast, but still make an impact on consumers' attention. They are simply "there" – hence the term ambient. Media like milk bottles and milk cartons, the backs of bus tickets, the backs of parking tickets, shopping trolleys, and so on are worth a considerable amount of advertising revenue each year.

Your brief is to devise (and suggest a price for) a new ambient medium that will offer coverage to one of the following elusive but lucrative target markets:

a) Males aged 14-18.
b) Students.
c) Frequent flyers.

Activity 10.6

CASE STUDY – Dome and gloom?

The Millennium Dome will go down in history as one of the great marketing misfires of the century. Yet almost 6.5 million people visited it – making it the most popular attraction in the UK by some way in the year 2000. Over 80% of visitors were highly pleased by their experience. The Dome included cutting-edge interactive exhibits, world-beating technology and customer service of the highest standard, from a committed and genuinely enthusiastic staff.

So what was it that turned such an apparent triumph into an unmitigated media disaster? The Dome offered a unique challenge for marketing communications from the outset. Business sponsorship had to be negotiated in advance on the strength of an attraction that did not exist. Advance consumer marketing was hampered by the fact that the contents of the Dome were a closely guarded secret. Without a clear message to communicate to either sponsors or consumers, the early publicity was woolly and unconvincing. The original advertising campaign (aired on TV in December 1998) featured images of Easter Island accompanied by a rather solemn voice-over from Jeremy Irons about the achievements of humanity in the last 1000 years. Hardly the stuff to get the family's pulse racing.

The marketing team expected enthusiastic word of mouth to drive sales once the attraction opened, but this was drowned out early on by an antagonistic media for whom Dome-baiting became a source of easy headlines. Typical of the regular stories that newspapers ran was a report of a party of Japanese tourists who visited a nearby circus in Greenwich by mistake, and left convinced they had seen the Dome! Management changes, outrageous financial revelations, flamboyant resignations, and the replacement of the English Chief Executive of the New Millennium Experience Company by a French EuroDisney manager continued to feed the media's hunger for headlines. Yet the Dome held back from fighting the negative coverage out of a sense that they would never be able to beat the media at their own game.

Press, poster and television advertising tried to accentuate the positive instead, backing the promise of this once-in-a-lifetime experience with the strapline "One Amazing Day". Family audiences in particular were targeted with ticket deals and an advertising campaign called "Jaw Dropping", which featured a child visitor literally amazed by what he was seeing. By mid-year visitor targets were revised from the original wildly optimistic 12 million, to an achievable 6 million, and a sense of reality began to descend on the Greenwich fun palace. This was accompanied by a more aggressive posture towards the negative coverage. A new series of television advertisements were aired in July 2000, featuring three different commercials with the same theme – don't be a sheep! One showed a man dismissing Cuba as a holiday resort because he had never been there, another showed a couple rejecting a waiter's recommendation in a restaurant because they had never tried it before, but the most hard-hitting featured a number of people dressed as sheep who had made up their minds not to go to the Dome.

This new attitude seems to have paid off. In October, three months before its planned closure, the Dome saw its first profitable month (ignoring earlier debts). By contrast, EuroDisney was open for three years before it turned a profit.

Perhaps a more vigorous marketing communications reaction earlier to negative media coverage might have helped restore the Dome's fortunes in time. But in spite of its saucer shaped structure, it was always going to be a hard mountain to climb!

Questions

1. Brainstorm some techniques to encourage journalists to take a positive view of a new visitor attraction.

2. What risks were the Dome's marketing team taking by trying to counter the negative publicity surrounding their attraction by running the Baa! campaign? Do you agree with their decision to do so? Comment on its timing.

3. Debate the respective merits of posters, television and press as advertising media for the Dome in attracting the family market.

Source

Kleinman, M. (2000) 'What did the Dome do for us?', *Marketing,* 21 December, p15.

SUMMARY OF KEY POINTS

- AIDA (Attention, Interest, Desire and Action) provides a flexible and useful model of communication, although reality is considerably more complex.

- Push promotion focuses on getting channel intermediaries to stock the product, pull promotion focuses on creating demand from end-users.

- Advertising is a good way of long-term brand building, but is expensive and takes place in a cluttered environment.

- Press relations often result in highly credible communications for your brand, but are difficult to control.

- Sales promotion is often effective in the short term, but doubts have been raised about its long-term benefits.

- Personal selling is extremely powerful as a communications tool, but needs careful management because of its expense.

- The Internet allows a high degree of personalisation and interactivity.

Glossary of terms

above the line: promotional activity through paid media.

advertising: paid-for media communication designed to inform and influence existing or potential customers.

AIDA: Attention, Interest, Desire, Action.

banner ad: a portion of a web page used to carry advertising. Often features animation and an active link to the advertiser's own web site (see click-through).

below the line: promotional expenditure that is not through paid media, commonly used to describe sales promotion expenditure.

click-through rate: the percentage of people seeing an Internet banner advertisement who use it as a link to carry them to the advertiser's web page.

cookies: small text files which are left on the hard drive of your computer when you visit a web site (to help identify you should you visit again, so that it knows your preferences). Some people object to cookies on privacy grounds, but many web sites will not work properly if you set your browser not to receive them.

coverage: the percentage of your target audience reached by your advertising.

frequency: the number of times on average a member of your target audience is reached by your advertising.

HTML: HyperText Mark-up Language – the language in which web pages are written in order to be visible to web browsers. Hypertext allows you to jump from one page to another through active links.

Internet Protocol (IP) number: the unique number that identifies each computer connected on the web.

Internet Service Provider (ISP): an organisation with a server, through which its customers connect to the Internet. ISPs tend to offer packages including access to the World Wide Web, space on their servers for their customers' web sites, and email addresses.

Intranet: an internal web site that is not accessible to people outside a defined group. Intranets usually exist inside a particular organisation and contain documents, discussion/notice areas and official information.

marketing communications: the process of informing and persuading the market of the benefits of a product or service (also known as "promotion").

media: vehicles which carry advertising; such as press, television, Internet, cinema, radio and posters.

pop-ups: promotional web pages that download automatically between the pages actually sought by a user. Intrusive and potentially very irritating.

portal: a web site that specialises in leading you to other web sites. Portals are often specific to a particular industry or leisure interest and are a useful source of advertising revenue.

press relations: encouraging the media to report positively on your products or your organisation.

public relations: the management of mutual understanding by an organisation with its publics.

pull strategy: promotional activity which aims to stimulate demand in customers, to "pull" goods through the distribution system.

push strategy: promotional activity which targets distribution intermediaries, in order to "push" goods through the system.

sales promotion: promotional activity designed to increase the speed or volume of transactions.

selling: interpersonal activity that facilitates the purchase of goods and services.

server: a computer which can be accessed by other computers, either on a network or the Internet. Like a waiter it "serves" up files (such as web pages) to other computers.

spam: the email version of junk mail – unwanted and sometimes troublesome email.

Wireless Application Protocol (WAP): a system that allows mobile phones and digital personal assistants (e.g. Palm organisers) to connect to the Internet through radio waves rather than cables.

Self-test multiple-choice questions

1. **The AIDA model suggests that effective advertising ends in:**
   a) Attraction.
   b) Anticipation.
   c) Action.
   d) Affiliation.

2. **Pull promotion concentrates on which of the following?**
   a) Wholesalers.
   b) Retailers.
   c) Resellers.
   d) Consumers.

3. **The percentage of a target group reached by your advertisement at least once is known as:**
   a) Frequency.
   b) Ambience.
   c) Coverage.
   d) Consistency.

4. **Which one of the following is not an advantage claimed by Press Relations as a marketing communications technique?**
   a) Cost-effectiveness.
   b) Control.
   c) Credibility.
   d) Audience reach.

5. **A click-through rate is:**
   a) A measure of success for banner advertising.
   b) A type of Internet search engine.
   c) A price charged by an Internet Service Provider.
   d) The speed at which an Internet user moves from web page to web page.

Something to think about...

1. Argue the case for using advertising rather than public relations in the following situations: publicising a new television series, promoting car insurance, selling a house.

2. Take two sales promotions you have noticed recently on products with which you are familiar (e.g. "Free Books for Schools" with crisps and newspapers, and "Buy One, Get One Free" with toiletries). How does the choice of promotion reflect the marketer's idea of the Decision-Making Unit in each case (see Session 5)?

3. Are there any products or services that are so popular, or so necessary, that they do not need promotion?

4. Discuss the proposition that selling skills are fundamental to success in an organisation, even if you never meet an external customer.

5. In what ways does a web site differ from a brochure?

Session 11

Marketing in context: Services

The essential approach to marketing is the same in both service and manufacturing-based industries. After all, customers are only interested in benefits, not in whether they are buying a physical product or an intangible service. But this Session will discuss some of the important practical emphases in service marketing which spring from the characteristics of services.

LEARNING OUTCOMES

At the end of this Session you should be able to:

- Identify and illustrate some important differences between products and services.

- Discuss the role of the customer in service provision.

- Give a basic explanation, with examples, of pricing in service markets such as air travel.

- Offer examples of how promotion and distribution work in service markets.

STUDY TEXT

We now spend more money on services than on goods in the UK. Entertainment, education, healthcare and holidays are all booming markets. The service economy has been boosted by the rapid growth of new industries like mobile telephones, software and computer games, and greater competition in existing ones like transport, financial services and power supply. All of these industries have something in common. Instead of delivering customer benefits through supplying physical goods they perform services. Understanding services, and marketing them accordingly, is therefore crucially important in contemporary business.

Services are different from goods insofar as they have no physical attributes. Admittedly, services are often delivered through a physical device, such as a television set or a cash machine, but it is the programmes or the convenient access to money and account information that provides the customer benefits. The physical side of the arrangement is incidental. Marketing theorists point to four main ways in which services differ from physical goods. These are known as service characteristics:

- Intangibility.
- Difficulty of like-for-like comparisons.
- The role of the customer in producing a service.
- Perishability.

Intangibility literally means unable to be touched. This refers to the fact that, unlike a physical good, you cannot put a service into a box, or hold it in your hand. This may seem a bit obvious, but it has the important consequence that it is impossible to know what a service is like before you try it. With a physical good there is the opportunity to examine something before purchase. You can taste a glass of wine before buying a case of it, or you can go for a test drive in a car to see how it handles. With services this is not the case. Once you commit yourself to having a haircut for example, there is no going back.

Service marketers have to bear this in mind, as it makes buying a service a high-risk operation. It is common therefore for service providers to offer prospective customers a trial version of the service before purchase. Software packages for example are often available on a 30-day trial basis, after which the full version must be purchased or the trial version ceases to work. Colleges often run taster sessions to give potential students a clearer idea of what to expect if they enrol on a course.

The difficulty of comparing like with like in service markets is sometimes referred to as **heterogeneity** – an unfamiliar word that just means differentness. In other words, services tend to be unique. With a mortgage or a pension you are faced with numerous choices, and deciding between all those available involves weighing up a number of complicated factors. Some might have lower regular payments than others, but with less flexibility in other ways. Some investment schemes are higher risk, but offer potentially higher returns than others that are safer but less spectacular. In the theatre no two productions, or even performances, of a play will ever be identical. Like intangibility, heterogeneity makes for a high degree of perceived risk on the part of buyers. This means that personal selling and customer advice are usually more important to the marketing of services than they are to the marketing of physical goods.

Physical goods are produced in factories, and then sold, often months later, to customers who may be on the other side of the world. Services, on the other hand, are produced wherever and whenever the customer uses them. Think of a visit to the bank – a common example of a service. The effective delivery of benefits to the personal banking customer depends on what the customer does as much as on what the bank does. Unless you know how to queue, what forms to fill in, and how to behave when you get to the counter, your experience is not likely to be satisfactory and you will not get your banking done properly. Of course the bank's side of the arrangement needs to be satisfactory too – and the better they serve you as a customer the more effective your participation will be. The key thing to remember is that services need both service provider and customer to make them happen, a characteristic that is sometimes referred to as **inseparability of production from consumption.**

Such active involvement of the customer in the production of a service has a number of marketing consequences. Educating customers into their part of the process is an important task for service providers. This is why even very young children are encouraged to accompany their families for dental check-ups – to get them used to the idea of sitting still with their mouths open for uncomfortable periods of time. In later life this should enable them to cope with visiting the dentist without panicking, and thus lead to more effective dental treatment when necessary. A more commercial example is IKEA, the Swedish furniture retailer that has managed to change the way we shop for beds and sofas. Furniture is of course a physical good. But retailing is a service, and IKEA's system of forcing customers to file through its hangar-sized showrooms before making their own selection of flat packs from the warehouse shelves involves its customers in service provision rather too deeply for some! It certainly takes a trip or two to get used to it as a way of shopping, but enough customers are happy to trade their personal inconvenience for IKEA's low prices to make it an international retailing success story.

Perishability is a fourth characteristic of services. Services cannot be stored. They are either used or they perish. You cannot, for example, only use half a hair cut and save the rest for later. If a train leaves the station only half full, the unsold seats remain unsold forever. Service marketers thus find themselves at a disadvantage compared to their colleagues who market physical goods. If you do not sell your expected volume of soap powder one week, you can always store the surplus and hope to sell it next week. You might even consider offering customers a discount in order to get rid of slow selling stock. But service providers have to aim to sell everything they supply immediately. They need to match supply to demand when and where it occurs.

This leads to pricing tactics that often seem very complicated. Service providers offer discounts in advance in order to tempt people to commit to purchase. An airline will offer a number of cheap seats on each flight that can only be booked a certain number of weeks in advance. Such bargain seats are sold under strict conditions – no refunds or changes are allowed. This guarantees the company its sales, and many travellers are willing to exchange flexibility for low prices. Other examples of pricing to match demand for services with supply are peak and off-peak rates for electricity or telephone calls.

Service marketing mix

Customers are not interested in whether an organisation is providing a physical good or a service. They are only interested in the benefits available. Essentially therefore, there is little difference between marketing a physical product and a service from the point of view of satisfying customer needs. However, there are some important operational differences in how service marketing is carried out. These result from the service characteristics examined in the previous section, some of which we have discussed already. A convenient way of summing them up and developing our understanding of them is to think of the marketing mix from a service point of view.

Product

Maintaining **service quality** is a major preoccupation in service marketing. We have seen that it is very difficult to make like-for-like comparisons between services, because no two are ever exactly the same. This means that service providers often struggle to ensure consistency of quality. With a physical good it is relatively easy to ensure consistency. Specifying how the product should be made and checking it for defects after manufacture means that customers can expect a product, like a can of beans, bought today to be virtually indistinguishable from the can of beans they bought last week. Services are potentially more variable. As a result many service providers have extremely clear guidelines on how their staff must carry out procedures. Burger King, for example, have an eight-step system which staff use in greeting the customer, taking their order, suggesting other purchases such as a drink or fries, handling money and thanking the customer. While being repeatedly told to "have a nice day" can sound a bit mechanical, at least systems like these ensure that all customers receive a minimum standard of cordiality and efficiency.

Activity 11.1 Mystery shoppers

Many service-providing firms use what are known as mystery shoppers to check up on how they are doing by visiting their facilities as ordinary members of the public. They then rate them on aspects of the experience in order to indicate areas for improvement. This exercise allows you to be your own mystery shopper.

Using a sheet of flip chart paper or similar, work either on your own or in a small group, to make a flowchart of the different steps involved in receiving one of the following services:

- Visiting a bank in order to deposit a cheque.

- Visiting a restaurant for a romantic dinner.

- Visiting a betting office.

The easiest way of doing this is to visualise yourself outside the branch and go through the process of entering, carrying out the transaction step by step, and coming out again. Don't get too bogged down in detail! Eight to ten steps are sufficient for this exercise.

Next rate each step on a scale of 1 to 5, where 1 means poor and 5 means excellent, for how satisfactory you found the experience. It could be that the atmosphere and queuing system in the bank are excellent, but that the forms are confusing and the member of staff you deal with is unfriendly. The exercise should give you some idea of how the bank, restaurant or betting office can improve its service.

Activity 11.2 Customer scorecard

On your own, repeat the "customer score card" exercise given in Activity 11.1 (above). This time, however, put yourself in the shoes of one of your own customers. It might be someone at your workplace or at a part-time job, it might be your course tutor, it might even be a member of your family! What are you like to deal with as a service provider?

Also read Hill and O'Sullivan (2004) *Foundation Marketing* (3rd Edition) FT/Prentice Hall, pages 33-38, 293-295 and self-check questions 6, 7 and 13 on pages 56-57.

Price

Services often have complicated pricing arrangements that offer different prices at different times. This is known as **differential pricing,** because different prices are charged to different segments of the market, depending on their usage pattern. Landline telephone pricing is a good example of this, where making calls during the day costs considerably more than in the evening or at weekends. This ensures revenue maximisation – in other words, the customers most able to pay (businesses) are soaked for the maximum price at the times when they need to use the service most. After the working day, however, telephone companies are left with excess capacity. This is when they offer evening and weekend rates to encourage private individuals to use the services that would otherwise go to waste.

Pricing for mobile telephone users is even more complicated, with the exact price of calls geared to a pre-determined pattern of usage. Mobile users can take out a contract for a particular tariff – a pricing system that reflects their likely patterns of use. Thus callers who expect only to use their phones in an emergency choose a tariff which allows them to pay low rental but high call charges, but those who expect to use their phones a lot will pay higher rental but low call charges. Indeed, they may even be entitled to a number of free calls as part of the deal. While such contracts might ensure that telephone companies can predict the capacity required, and thus match supply to demand, many consumers are wary of being tied into inflexible contracts. As a result, there has been a massive growth in the "pay as you go" market, where consumers, many of them in their early to late teens, are happy to buy pre-paid call time vouchers at prices which are higher per call than a regular contract would offer, but allow them much more flexibility.

Another pricing tactic associated with service marketing is **price bundling.** This involves pricing services as part of a package rather than individually. The advantage for both buyer and seller is that such an approach avoids the complexity of differential pricing. Not only is it easier to understand, but it often contains a bargain element which helps the seller move volume and the buyer get good value. Season tickets to football clubs are a good example of this. The ticket allows the buyer to attend regularly at a substantial discount compared to the single-ticket buyer. Most season tickets not only bundle together all the home matches for a season, but also include other service privileges such as access to other match tickets at a discount, or to social facilities. Another good example of price bundling in service industries is the package holiday. Instead of buying each element of the holiday separately, the tourist buys a package that offers less choice but far more convenience.

Activity 11.3 The right price?

Rajesh Patel sells new and second-hand computers from his shop in Bradford. He has a workshop upstairs where two part-time computer engineers carry out repairs. The engineers are paid £9 an hour, but they are not guaranteed work every day. This suits them as they are students at the local university and study is their first priority. Customers bring their faulty equipment into the shop and leave it for an estimate to be carried out. Rajesh looks at the job and decides in advance how many hours it will take, and how much any new parts will cost. The parts are the easy bit – the trick is to get the number of hours of labour right. Sometimes it is clear that a repair would be uneconomical, and it would be cheaper just to buy a new machine. There is a flat charge for the estimate of £25, which is then deducted from the total cost of the repair if the customer decides to go ahead with the job. All prices include VAT.

More often than not the price Rajesh quotes turns out to be correct, but sometimes he gets it wrong. One of his worst memories is of a job that took four times as long as he originally thought and on which he lost nearly a thousand pounds. Usually the mistaken estimates balance out over time – some in his favour, some in the customer's favour.

However, Rajesh is beginning to have doubts about his pricing strategy. A new computer superstore has opened up on the outskirts of town offering free estimates for repairs. After all, their advertising claims, why should you the customer pay if you decide not to have anything done? Rajesh does not agree with the logic of this argument, but a number of his customers have pointed it out to him lately.

What would you advise him to do?

Promotion

As well as advertising and sales promotion (for example free child places on package holidays), services rely heavily on **editorial public relations** in their promotional activities. This is a result of the high perceived risk of services, due to their intangibility, and the inseparability of their production from their consumption. In other words, it is practically impossible to know what a service is like before you have committed yourself to experiencing it. So how do you know whether it is likely to be a dud or not? Going on holiday to an unfamiliar destination, seeing a play by an unknown author, trying a new restaurant. All are situations where customers face an unknown quantity. Word-of-mouth recommendation from someone who has already had the experience is a strong encouragement to take a gamble on something new. Because of the need to reach large numbers of customers however, service providers cannot rely on personal word of mouth alone. They have to deal with professional intermediaries to spread the message. As a result, tourist destinations offer travel journalists free holidays, or theatres offer critics free seats, in the hope of a favourable review. This reliance on third-party recommendation explains the importance of editorial public relations to many service industries such as entertainment, restaurants, financial services and tourism.

In services markets such as finance or travel, many of the products on offer are complex and difficult to describe. Customers may be very confused by the range of options available. This explains why **personal selling** is an important part of most services promotional mix. It also explains the popularity of **umbrella branding** in many services markets, where the assurance of quality and reliability for individual products is created by an overall image. This allows a simple message to be applied to many complex products.

Place or distribution

Services cannot be stored. Furthermore, they are produced when and where they are used. This means that distribution techniques like transport or warehousing, which are applied to physical goods, are irrelevant to services. On the other hand, if we take distribution to mean creating the most effective and economical access to our service for consumers, then it becomes very relevant indeed. Time and location are the crucial factors here. When does the customer need the service and where should it be available?

Service providers can gain competitive advantage by supplying their services at convenient times. Convenience stores take their name from the fact that they offer extended opening hours compared with other grocery outlets. Major supermarkets have responded by establishing virtually round-the-clock opening times in some stores, but there are still a number of restrictions which do not apply to their smaller but more convenient rivals. Banks are another service industry where time-related distribution changes have been a significant competitive factor in recent years. Some branches have offered extended opening hours, but most importantly the growth of Automated Telling Machine (ATM) networks has made services such as cash availability, deposit facilities and account information available on a 24-hour a day basis for many customers.

Timing can also help limit the availability of what is on offer, so that service providers are never left with spare capacity. Ferry services between certain UK ports and Ireland only operate at certain times of the year, to reflect the heavy demand from holidaymakers. When there is less demand the ferry link stops, leaving passengers to find alternative ways of making their journey. This means that permanent or full-time jobs in service industries are rare. Many service industries such as tourism, catering and software, rely on a large number of casual workers, who are employed for only part of the year.

Activity 11.4 Growing success

A friend of yours is setting up in business as an independent landscape gardener. She has heard that you are studying marketing, and asks you for some advice on how to promote her new service to the right kind of customers.

Write her a short letter of no more than 250 words, outlining some useful recommendations.

The three extra Ps of the marketing mix

Marketing theorists have extended the familiar formula of the four Ps to include three further variables especially relevant for service marketing: people, process and physical evidence.

People

Most services are dispensed by people to people. The exceptions are examples of routine automation such as ATMs or telephone queuing systems. Even so, these need human back up. As a result of the human factor, investment in staff recruitment and development is particularly important to successful service marketing. Customers identify the organisation with its visible representative, so staff involved in service delivery need to be able to make decisions and take personal responsibility for quality.

Process

As we have seen, customers themselves are partners in service delivery. The quality of their experience is improved greatly by how comfortable they are with the step-by-step process involved. Simplifying unnecessarily complicated aspects of a service is one way of improving process. Telephone or Internet booking facilities for concerts or exhibitions save customers the inconvenience of queuing in person. Ticketless air travel reduces costs for budget airlines, which means lower prices for passengers. Even the design of a form can make a considerable difference to customer satisfaction, and thus to repeat business.

Physical evidence

Also known as physical environment, this extra P acknowledges the intangibility of services. While the service itself has no tangible features, the environment in which it is delivered has. Managing the physical evidence of a service, i.e. the features of its physical environment, can be a powerful source of competitive advantage. Uniforms worn by air cabin crew for example not only help identify them but reassure passengers of their professionalism. This is important in an industry where perceived safety is high on the list of customer requirements. Decor, atmosphere, even temperature, all put customers at their ease and contribute to a satisfactory service experience.

Activity 11.5 Good form!

The telephone is one of the most powerful business service technologies ever invented. However, because we are so familiar with it, we tend to take it for granted. Here are a few ideas to improve your telephone skills at a stroke.

- Always keep a pen and pad near the telephone.
- Try smiling or using gestures when you are on the telephone – it makes an audible difference, as does standing up to answer the phone (to make you sound more alert!).
- Group calls together at a particular time in the day.
- Prepare an agenda for each business call, perhaps just a list of points you need to discuss, and keep to it.
- Try to set a mental time limit on each call.

This exercise requires you to design a form (a typical piece of physical evidence in many service situations) to be used as a telephone message pad. When you have drawn one up, either by hand or using a word processor, exchange it with another student for comment.

Activity 11.6

CASE STUDY – AOL in the UK

From its humble beginnings as one of the first companies inspired by the commercial possibilities of the Internet back in 1985, America Online (AOL) has developed into a leading Internet Service Provider (ISP). On the way it has absorbed a number of other businesses such as Netscape, Compuserve and the media giant Time Warner. But for all the global reach of such a business, whose interests range from web access through e-commerce to films and publishing, the competitive focus of the company around the world is on local markets.

The very name AOL, with its connotations of American domination of the web, is not the most convenient branding device for international markets. However, by concentrating on the initials rather than the words behind them, and by forming national subsidiaries with strong local identities, the company promotes considerable autonomy in its international operations.

AOL UK, the subsidiary company in the UK, faces rapid environmental change. Since its 1995 launch, a number of rivals have entered the market and then collapsed. As access to the web increases at home, customers are looking not only for efficiency and reliability, but also for interesting content from their Internet providers, as well as demanding rock-bottom prices for net surfing. The merger with Time Warner should guarantee that AOL will be able to offer its customers plenty of interesting things to look at. Its mixture of information and entertainment should guarantee a high level of "stickiness" – the ability to keep customers loyal to a particular site. The stickier a site is, the more attraction it holds for advertisers. But the key to getting UK users to think of the Internet as just another medium (like the television or radio) is unmetered access.

Unmetered access, which US consumers take for granted because of how their telephone companies operate, gives net surfers unlimited time online for a flat charge. Traditionally, British Telecom has only offered ISPs like AOL second by second billing for use of their phone lines, thus making US-style access prohibitively expensive. In May 2000 the regulating authorities forced BT to conclude "wholesale" deals with ISPs, allowing them to pass on their savings to customers. This had the advantage of allowing customers to surf happily, safe in the knowledge that they are not running up massive phone bills. In fact the then market-leading ISP in the UK, Freeserve, had already amassed colossal debts by being the first into the market with unmetered access, subsidising the cost itself. Whilst this had given Freeserve a head start, many potential customers were frustrated by the service being oversubscribed and continued to be wary about "free" access promises.

AOL UK sees the way to achieve market dominance is to constantly update what it is offering and careful market segmentation based on offering different levels of service and prices. AOL UK also hopes to gain an advantage through its international network of companies and allies, in order to facilitate access to its web-based services for customers anywhere in the world.

Questions

1. How does AOL UK segment its market?

2. Discuss the advantages of flat-rate pricing for Internet access. Could this way of pricing be usefully applied to other services that are currently priced on a pay as you go basis?

3. Internet-based entertainment and information services such as AOL UK are competing against established media such as newspapers and broadcast media. What can web-based services offer customers that their traditional media rivals cannot?

Sources

Mazur, L (2001) "Keeping it Local", *Marketing Business,* December/January, pp6-18.

SUMMARY OF KEY POINTS

- Services differ from physical goods because of their intangibility, heterogeneity, perishability and inseparability of production from consumption.

- A typical services marketing mix will place great emphasis on: service quality; pricing and distribution which matches supply to demand; and promotion which helps customers understand what they are buying and reduces perceived risk.

- Service marketers often talk about the three "extra Ps" of people, process and physical evidence.

Glossary of terms

differential pricing: charging different prices to different segments of the market.

heterogeneity: the characteristic of services which means that no two service experiences will be identical.

inseparability of production and consumption: the characteristic of services which means that the customer is an integral part of the service delivery.

intangibility: the characteristic of services which means that they cannot be inspected or tried before purchase.

people: the employees involved face to face in delivering services.

perishability: the impossibility of storing services.

physical evidence: the environment in which services are delivered.

price bundling: pricing a package of services or goods rather than offering individual items at individual prices.

process: the systems designed to deliver services.

umbrella branding: bringing a number of products or services under a common brand image.

Self-test multiple-choice questions

1. **Services are difficult to try out before purchase because of their...**
   a) Intangibility.
   b) Imperishability.
   c) Integrity.
   d) Impenetrability.

2. **The systems designed to deliver services are known as...**
   a) Product.
   b) Process.
   c) Place.
   d) People.

3. **Staff uniform is an example of which aspect of service marketing?**
    a) People.
    b) Process.
    c) Physical evidence.
    d) Product.

4. **Offering a set price for a combination of services and/or physical goods is known as...**
    a) Price lining.
    b) Price bundling.
    c) Price discrimination.
    d) Price sensitivity.

5. **Consider the following two statements in relation to services.**

    i)   **Service perishability means that services often have complicated pricing.**
    ii) **Third party endorsement, for example by journalists, is an important aspect of promotion in many service markets.**

    Which of these is true?
    a) i only.
    b) ii only.
    c) both i and ii.
    d) neither i nor ii.

Something to think about...

1. How might someone wanting to improve their fitness choose between a product-based solution (such as buying an exercise video) and a service-based solution (such as joining a fitness centre)?

2. What advice would you offer one of the following businesses on how to give their customers a better service experience: a dentist, a betting office, a train operating company.

3. Telephone selling is becoming an increasingly popular part of service marketing. What are the disadvantages of this form of promotion in markets such as insurance or travel?

4. How does the decor of a bank contribute to your feeling of trust or security as a customer?

5. When is the best time to advertise holidays?

Session 12

Marketing in context: Not-for-profit, International, and Industrial (Organisational) Marketing

Marketing's usefulness extends beyond consumer goods and services to other situations, such as business-to-business, not-for-profit and international marketing. Perhaps you work in one of these areas and have felt a bit neglected by the predominantly consumer focus of the Sessions so far. If so, perhaps the ideas here will help you understand the contribution marketing makes to your organisation.

LEARNING OUTCOMES

At the end of this Session you should be able to:

- Recognise and justify marketing activity by non-profit organisations.

- Explain the trend towards international marketing and identify some frequent barriers to the process.

- Describe a selection of international market entry methods.

- Outline and account for a typical industrial (organisational) marketing mix.

STUDY TEXT

Not-for-profit marketing

In spite of marketing's association with increasing profitability, some of the most successful marketing taking place today is carried out by organisations for whom profit is irrelevant. Such organisations include theatres, museums, schools, colleges, hospitals, even charities and churches. They are all members of the non-profit sector.

Why are they interested in marketing? Simply because it can offer them a route to fulfilling their missions. If we replace the idea of "profit" with the idea of "organisational objectives" (realising that for commercial organisations the two are practically synonymous) we can begin to see why marketing makes sense for non-profit organisations. All organisations have customers. Marketing is a business philosophy that sees customer satisfaction as the key to success. Therefore, all organisations should be able to benefit from marketing. Instead of increasing its profits, customer focus can make a non-profit organisation, like a charity, both more efficient and more effective.

Marketing co-ordinates the activities of the organisation towards the customer. As a result, use of resources becomes more efficient. In addition, the focus marketing places on planning and working towards clear objectives should make the organisation more effective. Marketing encourages organisations to be clear about who their customer groups are, and to think about their relationships with them in terms of an exchange between suppliers and buyers. This leads to a clearer idea of priorities, which helps guide action, and provides a basis for monitoring and evaluating progress.

For all its advantages however, marketing is often viewed with suspicion by people in non-profit organisations. This is for two main reasons. Firstly, marketing can be seen as unnecessary and wasteful. If a charity is arguing that it needs funds to do vital work, how can it justify expenditure on sophisticated publicity materials or advertising campaigns? The answer here is that those materials or campaigns may be key to the plan to increase fund-raising income or raise awareness. They are likely to have been chosen as the most cost-effective route available. The other, more fundamental, reason for suspicion of marketing amongst not-for-profit workers, is that marketing is seen as manipulative, and therefore unethical for use in situations like education, health or the arts. The popular image of advertising and marketing as playing on our insecurities to help make a quick buck for unscrupulous entrepreneurs is to blame for this. The answer here is that any powerful tool can be used unethically by unscrupulous people, but that the fault lies in the user rather than in the tool. Marketing is neither morally good nor bad in itself – it is what you do with it that matters.

Fundamentally, marketing, as used by non-profit organisations, is the same process as that used by the commercial sector. But, as we shall see in this Session, the emphases of the marketing mix in this context has a particular flavour to it. Product in most not-for-profit organisations is often about providing customers with opportunities to achieve their own benefits, rather than just supplying them direct. Think of the example of education. Students are given opportunities to learn and be assessed, not simply handed a qualification in return for money. Non-profit organisations often supply their customers with what the organisation thinks they need in the long term, rather than what the customers think they want at the time. This is not such an outrageous marketing idea when you consider that commercial companies launching new products are often in a very similar position, offering customers things they don't yet realise they need (who would have thought people needed text messaging!).

Price in not-for-profit marketing is often expressed in non-financial terms. Even when money is involved (as in theatre tickets or tuition fees) prices are frequently subsidised to encourage take-up. Time or inconvenience are also common elements of non-profit pricing. Time is what volunteers in a charity shop pay for the benefits of feeling they are helping others, and their sense of well being. The final customers of the charity, the recipients, pay for it not with money but with time and co-operation in the funded projects.

Place or distribution is an important consideration for non-profit organisations. Location and timing of delivery is key (as in all service marketing), and often non-profit organisations will go out of their way to reach customers. Local authority library departments, for example, run mobile library services to reach users in locations remote from branch libraries. Equality of opportunity to participate in services, such as education or healthcare, is often a central objective in this sector, and is reflected by policies on issues like disabled access. Indeed, this is an area where commercial sector marketing is having to catch up with many non-profit organisations as a result of changing legislation.

Finally, promotion in non-profit organisations has some interesting emphases. Usually, but not always, it avoids high-cost techniques such as advertising. The exception is when a charity, for example, runs a campaign in order to raise awareness of an issue. Even so, steps are often taken to demonstrate to the target audience that the organisation is not squandering money. The NSPCC's award-winning recent campaign drew attention to child abuse, and featured poster and television advertising carrying sponsor credits for Microsoft as bearing the cost of the media. Similarly, many advertising agencies offer their creative and media planning services free to a selected charity, as a form of sponsorship in kind. Editorial PR, direct mail (for targeted fund-raising) and printed materials are common promotional tools for non-profit organisations, because of their cost-effectiveness. Another consequence of the equal opportunities outlook of many non-profit organisations is the determination to avoid stereotypes or condescending imagery in promotional material.

Activity 12.1 Being charitable

Charities often make an extra push at Christmas when donors are feeling well disposed to mankind in general. The Copgrove Theatre Trust has just carried out such an appeal, spending £38,000 on mailing almost 70,000 donors on its database with a Christmas card and details of its award-winning work with children's drama. The Trust's Marketing Manager has segmented the database into four segments. Active donors, who have already given cash in the last 24 months, but have no regular commitment. Gift Aid donors, who are taking advantage of a government-sponsored scheme to give tax-efficiently. Regular donors, who use standing orders to give money, and lapsed donors, people who have given in the past, but not for two years.

The results of the appeal have been gratifying, not just for the money brought in, but also for the information on which type of donors give what. This exercise invites you to use a spreadsheet to make sense of the data. The spreadsheet this is based on is Microsoft Excel, but other packages offer similar features, so you should be able to adapt the instructions accordingly.

	Total response	Total £	% resp.	Average donation	Income/ 1,000	Number mailed
Active cash donors	6,222	55,312.81				54,672
Gift aid donors	156	2,900.00				2,031
Standing orders	180	4,897.50				2,398
Lapsed donors	123	2,787.32				7,897
Totals	6,681	65,897.63				66,998

1. Create a spreadsheet containing the above data.

2. Enter formulae to work out the values for rows under the other columns as follows:

   - % response = (Total Response/Number Mailed)*100.

   - Average donation = Total £/Total response.

   - Income/1,000 = (Total £/Number Mailed)*1,000.

This last figure is a useful one. Even though the few lapsed donors who gave money gave generously (resulting in a high average donation), the vast majority of those mailed did not – raising doubts about the economy of mailing this part of the list.

3. Format the numerical cells to display decimals to one point (this can be done by highlighting the cells, choosing Format from the menu bar, and using the Cells option to alter the decimal places displayed by Number. Alternatively your screen display may be set to offer a button letting you do it more quickly).

4. Format the label cells at the top of the spreadsheet to display vertically rather than horizontally (again highlight the relevant cells, take the Format command, choose Cells and then Alignment to make your change).

5. Finally, highlight all the cells (holding down the Ctrl key with A should do this), select Format, Column, and AutoFit Selection, to display the spreadsheet elegantly.

Use the information created to discuss the following questions:

- Who are the most generous donors?
- What do the figures on lapsed donors suggest about how you might develop your fund-raising?
- Should you be concerned about the standing order figures?

International marketing

International marketing involves any marketing activity that crosses national boundaries. As the world becomes more connected through Information and Communication Technology and easier travel, there are few organisations whose marketing remains untouched by the international dimension. However, as with non-profit and organisational marketing, international marketing brings its own set of variations on how to put marketing principles into practice.

Activities that fall under this heading range from **exporting,** where a firm is clearly based in one country but sells its goods to customers internationally, to **global marketing,** where enormous companies produce and sell their products throughout the world, ignoring differences between customers in different countries and concentrating instead on the similarities between them in order to treat the world as a single market. Addressing international markets opens up access to large numbers of customers and potential sales, but it also introduces risks and difficulties on a different scale from those experienced by marketers limited to one country.

Reasons for internationalisation

There are a number of reasons why, in spite of the complexities and risks involved, companies internationalise their marketing. These range from conscious strategic decisions, taken in the light of changing macro- or micro-environmental conditions, to pure accident. Coca-Cola, one of the most famous examples of a global brand, owes its international presence not so much to any grand design, but to its policy of being available to American GIs around the world.

On the macro-environmental level there are plenty of factors driving the growth of international marketing. Socio-cultural changes, such as new eating habits stemming from consumers' experiences of foreign travel, have opened up international opportunities for food and wine producers. Technological shifts, such as the Internet, have effectively brought buyers and sellers in different countries closer together, making it easier to source products and services globally. Call centres and secretarial services can be anywhere in the world, so long as the customer is at the other end of the phone or fax line. Finally, economic and political changes, such as regional co-operation by groups of nations in trade zones (for example the burgeoning membership of the EU) have encouraged companies to respond by organising their marketing along similarly international lines.

On a micro-environmental level, competition in the domestic market can often squeeze profit margins so much that the only direction for a company to expand is abroad. Alternatively, a fall in the number of relevant customers in a particular national segment may force a manufacturer to spread its geographical net more widely. Intermediaries such as advertising agencies, and suppliers such as component manufacturers, have internationalised their businesses alongside their clients and customers. Consumers, the most important group of all, occasionally seem to be in danger of being left behind by this jamboree of internationalisation. For example, attempts to identify what might be called the "Euroconsumer" have floundered on important national differences. However, there are enough market segments where needs are similar (particularly in growth areas such as technology and transport) to make internationalisation an unstoppable trend.

Activity 12.2 International understanding

International communication is often hampered by language problems, but sometimes not being able to understand someone's spoken language can lead to more of an insight into the importance of non-verbal communication and body language. In spite of cultural differences (for example, the closer you go to the Mediterranean, the more exuberant people's gestures tend to grow), there is a lot of non-verbal communication that we share with people of other nationalities.

Body language is not a series of individual gestures with specific meanings. Rather it can give a general impression of someone's state of mind. Someone who touches their face or hair a lot may be feeling self-conscious. Leaning forward in a conversation is often a sign of interest and involvement. Standing back with arms folded is a sign of withdrawal, whereas hands on hips with chin up and legs apart can give off signals of aggression. You can actually look and feel more approachable by standing or sitting with a comfortable, open posture. Try observing people who put you at ease to see if there are any lessons about body language you can learn from them and practise yourself when you get a chance.

Also, read Hill and O'Sullivan (2004) *Foundation Marketing* (3rd Edition) FT/Prentice Hall, Not-for-Profit: pages 45-50; International Marketing: 373-400; Industrial/Organisational Marketing: pages 39-44 and 106-115, self-check questions 3, 4, 9, 11 and 12 on pages 56-57.

Market entry methods

Having made the decision to access a new international market, the next question is how to make an entry. This is a distribution or place decision, and it is one of the most crucial elements of any international marketing mix. The continuum stretches from low risk, low potential reward methods, such as exporting (where the company remains rooted in its domestic country), to high risk, high potential reward methods, such as foreign manufacture (where the company takes the risk of investing in the target country and manufacturing in the same country as its market). The level of potential losses from an unsuccessful entry are greater the more financial commitment the firm makes to the **host country**, the country in which the international marketing operations are to take place.

Activity 12.3 On the retail trail

New tourist destinations continue to open up all the time, as access to established resorts becomes ever easier. While some tourists never seem to get further than the beach and the hotel bar, many others enjoy seeing a bit of local life, and savouring the differences between the host country and their own. Shopping is one of the areas where this is most apparent. This exercise is about using the accumulated foreign shopping experience of your group in order to assemble a checklist of cultural differences between host countries.

First, working in small groups, assemble a checklist of shopping characteristics that might be different from home. Examples would include: typical size of shops, opening hours, standards of customer service, extent of specialisation, location, type or range of merchandise, etc.

Then in the wider group, choose a representative to make an overall list with characteristics (the most important five or six) down one side, and a number of countries across the top (limit this to the three most popular). In a general discussion, try to identify the types of retailing that offer customers something generally unavailable in your own country.

Then in your discussion consider whether there might be a business opportunity for imitating one of more of these in your own country, or whether the type of retailing is too dependent on local cultural circumstances.

Sometimes the price of admission exacted by the host country for access to its citizens as consumers is a measure of the commitment of the marketer. Anxious that the wealth created by the marketing activity should not just drain out of the economy back to the marketer's home country, some governments have insisted on **joint venture** agreements, whereby a new entrant to a national market has to join forces with a local firm in order to create employment opportunities. Such agreements are fine in principle, but often collapse after two or three years because of irreconcilable differences in management direction.

An alternative way of getting your brand into an international market is to license it to a local manufacturer. **Licensing** is an agreement whereby the owner of a product or an idea allows another company to use it in a foreign market in exchange for a royalty. Here the risk is minimal, at least in the short term, as the local manufacturer takes on manufacturing, distributing and marketing the product. The disadvantages are two fold. The first is that the returns for the licensor (the brand's original owner) are safe but minimal. The other is that the longer the local firm (the licensee) is involved in the deal, the more capable it is of developing a rival product once the agreement is over. However, for bulky products such as beer and soft drinks, licensing is a popular distribution method.

Barriers to international marketing

While the rewards for success are lucrative, there are plenty of obstacles that litter the path of the international marketer. Again, the familiar STEP factors can provide a useful framework for a brief consideration of some of them.

Socio-cultural differences are perhaps the key issue here, as they affect how customers in a particular country view your offer. Perhaps they have very pronounced local tastes that will prevent you from reaping the economies of scale available from product **standardisation** – the goal of marketing a single product acceptable to as many international customers as possible. In spite of the many similarities between consumers around the world, there are still important cultural differences in areas such as language, outlook, values and tastes, which make life difficult for the international marketer.

Technology, whilst opening up international opportunities in the shape of the Internet to many parts of the developed world, acts as a brake on international marketing in other areas. A good example is the technological infrastructure of transport. Poland has a good rail network but its roads currently fall short of the motorway standards of other European countries. An international marketer wanting to trade with Poland, but used to road transport as a mode of distribution, might therefore be disadvantaged by having to adapt to rail or endure delays. Technology also affects promotion. There are some promising new markets in developing countries where electricity supply happens to be patchy or television ownership sporadic. A manufacturer with a successful broadcast advertising strategy at home might have to start from scratch with a promotional strategy for the new market.

Economic issues also bedevil the international market. Movements in **exchange rates**, the relative values of currencies in different countries, can make your products hopelessly uncompetitive in price against local competition in the host country. The UK tourist industry, for example, has suffered like all British exporters from the recent strength of sterling relative to other currencies. It has meant that visitors from abroad get less for their money in an already high-cost country, and that UK tourists get even more for their money if they go abroad. Combined with unreliable weather, this does not create much of an incentive to holiday in Britain.

Politico-legal factors include product standards legislation and import taxes. Product standards are nominally there to protect consumers by guaranteeing safety or labelling features. They vary widely from country to country. To international marketers they sometimes appear to be a deliberate barrier to market entry, established less to protect local consumers from dangerous products than local businesses from foreign competition. The drive for common standards by the European Union is helping eradicate this difficulty within member states. Import taxes are a more direct form of protectionism, but can also be seen as a foreign government's legitimate reluctance to allow wealth to flow one way out of their economy.

Activity 12.4 Currency conundrum

Here is a list of international currencies, followed by how much they were worth on a particular day in 2000 compared to one euro. A word of caution, the higher the number the less 'valuable' the currency is per unit!

Czech Republic	Koruna	34.50
Denmark	Krone	7.51
Hungary	Forint	266.94
Poland	Zloty	3.57
Romania	Leu	24,887.10
Russia	Rouble	25.79
Japan	Yen	110.29
Indonesia	Rupiah	9,481.74
USA	Dollar	0.89
UK	Sterling	0.62

- How many Zloty are there to £1 sterling?
- How many US dollars will 5,000 Forint buy?
- How much is £1 worth in dollars?

Business-to-business marketing

Business-to-business marketing (or organisational marketing as it is sometimes known) accounts for a very significant amount of marketing activity. While the essential principle of customer satisfaction is still paramount, there are some important differences in emphasis between an organisational and a consumer marketing mix.

The main reason lies in the difference between organisational needs and consumer needs. Whereas consumers buy for themselves and their families' immediate use, **organisational buyers** are professionals who buy products and services on behalf of the organisations they work for. The organisations then convert the products and services into outputs that are sold on. The demand they express is called **derived demand**, because it follows on from demand for the products they produce for consumers. This means that if consumers stop buying jeans, garment manufacturers suddenly don't want denim any more, even if they have been your best customers. It also means that if consumers start buying jeans again, demand from organisational buyers will not die away, even if the price of denim goes up. Derived demand is relatively price inelastic.

Organisational buying behaviour differs from consumer buying behaviour because of this professional element. It is more rational and less impulsive. Organisational buyers are naturally conservative, and continuity of supply and quality are essential to them. Having said that, the buying roles identified in the classic marketing model established by Webster and Wind (1972) are very similar to the roles in a consumer Decision-Making Unit. The main difference is the role of gatekeeper – the person who controls the flow of information into the organisation. Getting past the gatekeeper, often a highly efficient personal assistant who prides themselves on protecting the boss from time-wasting sales calls, is the first hurdle for any organisational marketing approach. As with the consumer roles outlined in Session 5, more than one organisational buying role may be taken on by an individual, but they all need consideration in preparing a marketing and sales approach.

Figure 12.1

Organisational buying roles

- Gatekeeper.

- Decider.

- Buyer.

- Influencer.

- User.

Source: Webster and Wind (1972)

Although their approach to buying is more formal than that of consumers, organisational buyers' attitudes to their purchases vary in a way that parallels consumer behaviour. Just as consumers expend different amounts of time and care on different kinds of purchases (as discussed in Session 5), so organisational buyers vary their efforts according to how familiar or unfamiliar the buying task is.

The **straight rebuy** as it is known, is the routine purchasing of familiar supplies and services. It may be that this procedure is automated to a large extent, thus making it difficult for a new supplier to break into the process.

The **modified rebuy** on the other hand, presents more of an opportunity for a new supplier. Here the purchase is similar to what has been bought before, but the buyer will be looking for better quality, a higher specification, or a keener price.

The **new task** is the most stressful purchasing situation for an organisational buyer, because this covers the purchase of an unfamiliar good or service. Effective marketing and sales here can make life considerably easier for the buyer, and considerably more profitable for the supplier.

The business-to-business marketing mix

Using the familiar model of the four Ps can help us outline what makes organisational marketing different.

Product: quality is paramount because of the need to incorporate the incoming materials or parts into the production process. Many manufacturers now have quality agreements with their suppliers, where the responsibility for 100% quality is placed firmly on the shoulders of the suppliers.

Price: the advantage of such a heavy responsibility for quality inputs is that suppliers can charge a lot for them. At the end of the day, price is less of an issue in organisational marketing than in consumer marketing, because firms can pass on costs to their own customers (who in turn, research suggests, are prepared to pay for quality).

Promotion: one of the most noticeable differences between consumer and organisational marketing is in the choice of promotional techniques used. Whereas personal selling is the exception in consumer marketing, it is the rule in business to business, and is often accompanied by sales promotions such as quantity discounts. Furthermore, sales literature, such as brochures and illustrated catalogues, exhibitions and closely targeted press relations and advertising in specialist trade press, all assume an importance which sets this pattern of promotion apart from its consumer equivalent. The Internet has already assumed a central role in much business-to-business promotion because of its rapid adoption by organisations.

Place: distribution is also different from consumer marketing. Historically, businesses of a similar sort have tended to congregate in particular areas, because of the proximity of specific materials or energy sources. Even though the physical reasons for such clustering are less pressing now, there is still a trend towards linked businesses developing in proximity to one another (for example around science parks or innovation centres). Consumer outlets are, of course, much more widely dispersed.

Time is often a more crucial factor in organisational than consumer marketing. This is reflected in specialist distribution intermediaries who can get urgently needed parts or documents from place to place rapidly, at a price. Finally, business-to-business distribution often involves short marketing channels, with producers taking direct responsibility for delivery – especially of dangerous, bulky or highly valuable goods.

Activity 12.5 The write impression

Written communication is still essential to business-to-business transactions, in spite of our increasingly audio-visual world.

When we write a common mistake is to see things from our own point of view, when really we should be seeing things from the reader's point of view. We fall over ourselves to tell them what we have done, what we think, what we want them to know. But what do **they** want to know?

Think about it. Whenever you receive a letter or email the first question you ask is why is this person writing to me? This is usually followed by two further questions. What's in it for me? What do I have to do about it?

These three questions form the basis of a flexible model for written communications that will save you lots of time.

Why? 'I am writing to introduce myself as the new area representative for Copgrove Confectionery...'

What's in it for me? 'We are launching a new range of sophisticated luxury chocolate bars called the Copbana, and as one of our most valued past customers, I thought you might appreciate the opportunity to sample this exquisite product at an exclusive reception...'

What do I have to do? 'Please phone my secretary, Ms Desiree Parette, on the following number and confirm if you and a guest will be able to attend...'

Would that all business letters were that alluring, but you get the picture!

Now try it yourself. Write a letter of no more than one side of A4 on one of the following scenarios. When you have finished, find another student who has done the exercise and give each other feedback on your work. Also, try the technique on some real life correspondence this week.

- A letter to a business customer chasing an overdue £50 bill.

- A covering letter to a potential employer to accompany a job application for the post of marketing manager of a sportswear brand.

- A letter of complaint to a manufacturer of a faulty toaster.

Activity 12.6

CASE STUDY – Blowing the dust off museums

In the year 2000 American museums attracted over a billion visitors, their biggest visitor total to date. All around the world new museums are springing up, and the ones that are doing best, like London's Tate Modern and New York's Guggenheim, are the ones that are best at marketing. Not only are they pulling in crowds through the doors, but they also have substantial teams of fund-raisers, tapping new sources of income to supplement or replace dwindling state subsidies.

But traditionalists are worried that the show-business success of such innovatory venues is disguising the fact that museums are not just places to muse at masterpieces and interact with gadgets. Their primary role is the quiet, and rather boring, pursuit of conserving objects that are valued because of their cultural importance rather than their crowd-pulling power.

Mr Thomas Krens, head of the Guggenheim in New York, might disagree. Founded in 1939, his museum has become highly controversial recently with some very commercial exhibitions. 1998 saw an exhibition of motorcycles sponsored by BMW. Beautiful, maybe, but is it art? More controversially still, Autumn 2000 saw an exhibition of dresses designed by international fashion guru Giorgio Armani. Critics sniffed that the $15 million Armani donation to the museum that accompanied the show was more of a hire fee than a sponsorship.

Krens' other strategy is also brazenly commercial. He is extending the Guggenheim like an international franchise operation, along the lines of a high-culture Body Shop. There are already two branches in New York with a third underway, a Berlin branch opened in collaboration with Deutsche Bank, another in Venice and the famously curvy new Guggenheim in Bilbao. Las Vegas and Brazil are next on the list of locations. When complete the current expansion programme should double visitor capacity to 6 million a year – more than any other single US museum.

Other American museums have taken the hint, and there are currently 20 museums building new outlets in imitation of this exercise in brand extension. But there are also those who oppose the approach vehemently. One of Mr Kerns' most outspoken critics is Philippe de Montebello, who runs the ultra-traditional Metropolitan Museum in New York. His view is that the show business approach is doomed to failure because museums cannot compete with the likes of Disney, who are already offering this kind of experience to audiences. He feels so strongly about the importance of museums being independent from commercial influence that he cancelled a proposed exhibition of the work of the classic French designer Coco Chanel at the Met when Karl Lagerfield, the current head of Chanel, demanded to have an input into planning the show. Mr Montebello can afford his principles however. The Metropolitan Museum gets a much higher percentage of its annual running costs from the local authority than any other New York museum.

Questions

1. What are the benefits of a visit to an art museum? Is a modern museum like the Guggenheim offering different benefits from a more traditional museum like the Metropolitan, or are they broadly the same (in spite of their different features)?

2. A recent report claimed that London's Victoria and Albert Museum – once described as "The Nation's Treasure house" because of its vast collections of priceless objects – was being subsidised to the tune of £24 per visit, in spite of soliciting a £5 "donation" from each visitor. Make a brief argument either for or against the idea that this represents good value for the taxpayer. (It may depend on what you see as the role of museums.)

3. Are there any of the following organisations that you feel should not take commercial sponsorship (i.e. accept money in exchange for publicity and image benefits, such as a logo on a vehicle or uniform)? Justify your answer either way.

    - A primary school.
    - The police (sponsored vehicles).
    - The ambulance service.
    - A church running a roof appeal.
    - A counselling service with a 24-hour helpline.

Sources

Hill, L., O'Sullivan, C. & O'Sullivan, T. (2004) *Creative Arts Marketing,* 2nd edition, Butterworth-Heinemann.

The Economist (2001) 'When merchants enter the temple', *The Economist,* 21st April, pp87-90.

SUMMARY OF KEY POINTS

- Marketing can increase the effectiveness and efficiency of non-profit organisations.

- Non-profit organisations often display a concern for active rather than passive customers, non-financial pricing, and equal opportunities issues with regard to access and promotion.

- International marketing covers a wide range of activities from exporting to global marketing, along a continuum of low- to high-risk and reward.

- Factors in a firm's macro- and micro-environment can prompt it to enter new markets as a strategic response, or the entry may be an unconscious one.

- Business-to-business marketing responds to derived demand.

- Organisational marketing mixes display concern for quality over cost; a promotional mix that involves elements missing from the typical consumer equivalent; and patterns of distribution that tend to give suppliers more direct responsibility for delivery.

Glossary of terms

derived demand: demand for business products that originates from demand for consumer products.

exchange rate: the value of a country's currency in comparison with other countries.

exporting: manufacturing goods in one country, but selling them to customers internationally.

foreign manufacture: setting up international production facilities to serve international markets.

global marketing: treating the world as a single market by ignoring differences between customers in different countries and concentrating on similarities.

host country: the country in which international marketing operations take place.

international marketing: marketing activity that crosses national borders.

joint venture: collaboration between a domestic manufacturer and a foreign firm.

licensing: a low-risk form of market entry whereby the owner of a product or idea allows another company to use it in a foreign market in exchange for a royalty.

modified rebuy: purchase class for organisational buyer which involves a departure from a familiar purchase in some way.

new task: purchase class for an organisational buyer which involves a completely unfamiliar purchase.

not-for-profit sector: organisations that exist for reasons other than commercial gain.

organisational buyers: those who buy products and services on behalf of the organisations they work for.

standardisation: marketing a single product which is acceptable to as many international customers as possible.

straight rebuy: purchase class for an organisational buyer which involves routine rebuying of a familiar purchase.

Self-test multiple-choice questions

1. **Which of the following is a non-financial element of price?**
    a) Cash.
    b) Credit card.
    c) Time.
    d) Profit.

2. **International marketing activity that consists of a firm manufacturing in its own country and selling to customers internationally is known as:**
    a) Joint venturing.
    b) Licencing.
    c) Exporting.
    d) Global marketing.

3. In a licensing agreement, the firm that acquires the right to use or manufacture the idea or product at stake is known as:
    a) The licensee.
    b) The licensor.
    c) The licentiate.
    d) The license.

4. i) Derived demand displays price inelasticity.
    ii) Gatekeepers identify the need for new industrial purchases.

    Which of these is true?
    a) i only.
    b) ii only.
    c) both i and ii.
    d) neither i nor ii.

5. Which of the following is part of the economic environment for international marketing?
    a) Product standards legislation.
    b) Import tax.
    c) Exchange rates.
    d) Language barriers.

Something to think about...

1. Is marketing relevant to the prison service?

2. Take a charity with whose work you are familiar and list its different customer groups (try segmenting them by "benefits sought". See Session 6 on Behavioural Segmentation). Are there tensions between two or more groups? How does the charity resolve these tensions?

3. How might an understanding of pricing be useful to an organisation offering a free service to its customers?

4. Identify three market-entry methods that might be used by a company new to an international market.

5. Debate the idea that organisational buyers are more rational in their decisions than consumers buying for themselves and their families.

Appendix 1

The CIM Introductory Certificate Syllabus

Aims

The aims of the CIM Introductory Certificate in Marketing are to provide students who have little or no previous experience of marketing with the building blocks of marketing knowledge, by introducing the basic tools of marketing and exploring their use through studies of contemporary practice.

Objectives

The objectives of the CIM Introductory Certificate in Marketing are:

- To show how a range of environmental factors can influence how an organisation operates.

- To explore methods of research and information gathering and their relationship to marketing practice.

- To highlight the importance of understanding how customers make buying decisions, and the factors that affect those decisions.

- To help students identify target markets and use appropriate techniques for addressing those markets.

- To demonstrate how information and communications technology can be harnessed for use in marketing applications.

- To illustrate the application of marketing principles in a wide range of organisational contexts.

Learning Outcomes

When they have completed this course, students will be able to:

- ... identify the different factors that contribute towards developing a customer focused, marketing-led organisation.

- ... interpret and use basic marketing terminology.

- ... demonstrate an outline knowledge of ICT and its application to marketing.

- ... identify the key factors in organisations' micro- and macro-environments and describe why and how organisations respond to changes in these factors.

- ... explain the factors that can affect customers' buying decisions in a range of buying situations.

- ... gather and analyse simple data, from primary and secondary sources and communicate the findings.

- .... use market information to identify and evaluate potential market segments and justify targeting decisions.

- ... apply the marketing mix to optimise demand for products and services.

- ... distinguish between effective and ineffective tactics in a range of situations and contexts.

Outline content

Module One: The Essentials of Marketing

Marketing and the changing environment:

- What is marketing and its overall contribution and importance to the organisation **(5%)**.

- Planning for marketing activity; elements of a marketing plan and how they fit together **(5%)**.

- The marketing environment; the factors an organisation needs to consider; macro- and micro-environmental influences on businesses, including Information and Communications Technology **(10%)**.

Understanding customers:

- Customer relationships – understanding the influences on customers' behaviour, and the process of buying by consumers and organisations **(10%)**.

- Gathering information – identifying sources for and uses of marketing information, including secondary and primary marketing research **(10%)**.

- Target marketing – bases and criteria for market segmentation and approaches to market targeting **(10%)**.

Module Two: The Application of Marketing

The tools of marketing:

- Product – features and benefits, product life cycle theory, product mix and brands **(10%)**.

- Price – customer influences on price; financial considerations, including break-even analysis; and competitor considerations **(10%)**.

- Place – marketing channel issues; retailing; and e-commerce **(10%)**.

- Promotion – communication and the promotional mix, including e-marketing **(10%)**.

Marketing in Context:

- Key differences in marketing practice in a range of contexts: services, not-for-profit, international and business-to-business **(10%)**.

Syllabus detail

Module One: The Essentials of Marketing

1.1	Marketing and the changing environment	(20%)
1.1.1	*Marketing and its importance to the organisation.* ■ Definitions of marketing. ■ Marketing orientation and its alternatives. ■ The marketing concept and its implementation. ■ Reasons for the growth of marketing. ■ Future directions for marketing: societal marketing; relationship marketing.	**(5%)**
1.1.2	*Planning for marketing activity.* ■ Marketing audit. ■ SWOT analysis. ■ Marketing objectives. ■ Marketing strategies and tactics. ■ Marketing budgets.	**(5%)**

1.1.3	*The marketing environment.*	**(10%)**
	■ Socio-cultural factors.	
	■ Technological factors.	
	■ Economic factors.	
	■ Politico-legal factors.	
	■ Customers.	
	■ Competitors.	
	■ Suppliers.	
	■ Intermediaries.	
	■ Other stakeholders.	
1.2	**Understanding customers**	**(30%)**
1.2.1	*Customer behaviour.*	**(10%)**
	■ Differences between consumers and industrial buyers.	
	■ Influences on buyer decision making.	
	■ The decision-making unit.	
	■ The decision-making process.	
	■ Purchase classes.	
1.2.2	*Gathering information.*	**(10%)**
	■ Uses for marketing information.	
	■ Sources of secondary information.	
	■ Primary research; quantitative and qualitative, continuous and ad hoc.	
	■ Surveys; sampling; questionnaires; data collection (street, phone, mail, self-completion, web site, email).	
	■ Focus groups and depth interviews.	
	■ Observation and experiment.	

1.2.3	*Target marketing.*	**(10%)**
	■ Mass marketing, differentiated marketing, target marketing and niche marketing.	
	■ Geographic, demographic, psychographic and behavioural bases for market segmentation.	
	■ Criteria for effective market segmentation.	

Module Two: The Application of Marketing

1.3	**The tools of marketing**	**(40%)**
1.3.1	*Products (and services).*	**(10%)**
	■ Features and benefits.	
	■ Total product concept.	
	■ Product mix.	
	■ Product life cycles.	
	■ Brands.	
1.3.2	*Price.*	**(10%)**
	■ Pricing for profit (price skimming, premium pricing, differential pricing, auctions).	
	■ Pricing for volume (penetration pricing, discounting).	
	■ Cost influences on price (fixed and variable costs: break-even analysis).	
	■ Customer influences on price (price sensitivity, price elasticity).	
	■ Competitor influences on price.	
1.3.3	*Place.*	**(10%)**
	■ Marketing channels: types of intermediary.	

	■ Functions of agents, merchants, wholesalers and retailers.	
	■ Channel choice: selective, intensive and exclusive distribution.	
	■ E-commerce and distribution.	
	■ Physical distribution (order processing, materials handling, warehousing, inventory management and transport).	
1.3.4	*Promotion.* AIDA model of marketing communication. Push and Pull strategies. Uses, advantages and limitations of: ■ Advertising. ■ Editorial PR. ■ Sales promotion. ■ Selling. Internet (web sites; internet advertising).	**(10%)**
1.4	**Marketing in context**	**(10%)**
1.4.1	Services marketing (differences between products and services; characteristics of service provision). Not-for-profit marketing (differences from commercial marketing in terms of objectives and operational approaches). International marketing (reasons for going international; market-entry methods and barriers). Business-to-business marketing (differences from consumer emphases in marketing mix).	

Appendix 2

The CIM Introductory Certificate Assignment

In addition to the multiple-choice test that covers the whole syllabus, the two modules of the Introductory Certificate in Marketing (The Essentials of Marketing and the Application of Marketing) are assessed separately. Each one involves two pieces of written work (of up to 500 words each) – thus four pieces of work in all. This is a lot to ask – but you will find that the process of preparing and writing your answers will guarantee a thorough learning experience, and give you a qualification you can be proud of. The assignment questions require students to demonstrate their knowledge and understanding of marketing through applying their own experiences in work, or as a customer, to the marketing ideas covered by the syllabus.

As you progress through the course, you should be considering your every-day experiences of the application of marketing in each of the four sections of the syllabus:

Module One: The Essentials of Marketing

- **Marketing and the changing environment.**

- **Understanding customers.**

Module Two: The Application of Marketing

- **The tools of marketing.**

- **Marketing in context.**

The assignment questions for each module are designed to test your knowledge and understanding of the relevant section of the syllabus. Because this is an introductory marketing qualification, we have been careful not to assume any prior knowledge or professional experience of marketing as a condition of success in the assignment. As a result, the choice of questions for each section will always include one which offers candidates with little or no marketing experience the opportunity to display their knowledge and understanding of marketing, as well as one aimed at more experienced students. Of course, experience can include marketing in a voluntary capacity (for example for a club or society) every bit as much as in paid employment.

Because this is a marketing qualification, your answers need to use a report format rather than being discursive essays. Guidance on report writing is provided later in this appendix. For convenience we will refer to your assignment answers as "reports".

Preparation is the key to success for these assignments, and it is suggested that you take the following step-by-step approach.

1. Read the questions carefully and discuss them with the tutor to ensure you have a full and clear understanding of what is required.

2. Write a plan outlining how any tasks are to be approached.

3. Discuss possible ideas with the tutor and if necessary modify the plan.

4. Carry out the various steps in the assignment.

5. Produce a written report.

6. Prepare a presentation (if group work).

Your preparation can be conducted **either** individually **or** in groups. Either way, you must submit an individual report. Group members should avoid producing identical reports but should bring their own perspectives to the individual reports.

You should aim to be as concise as possible and submit between 400 and 500 words on each of the four questions across the two modules. Your report must have a logical structure, with clearly presented and explained sections, and have a clear, legible and business-like layout and format.

In an appendix to your report, you should include a record of the resources you used, such as:

■ Background reading.

■ Useful web sites.

■ Primary research undertaken.

Your report should be word-processed. Hand-written reports may be acceptable under certain circumstances, so if you are unable to submit a word-processed report you should discuss the reasons for this with your tutor.

Your presentation (group-work route only) should take no more than 20 minutes, and cover your answers to all four of the elements of the syllabus-related questions across the two modules. Your presentation must have a logical structure and be delivered in a clear business-like manner. Visual aids should be used where appropriate.

SAMPLE ANSWERS

In order to give you an idea of what you can expect in the assignment, we have provided a selection of specimen questions covering each section of the syllabus across both modules. Each is followed by a specimen answer, and a commentary which we hope will give you an idea of what we are looking for. The questions and answers are arranged by module and syllabus section. In each case there is a choice of question – (a) is aimed at less experienced candidates and can be answered perfectly satisfactorily with reference to your experience as a customer or from publicly available information, (b) assumes some direct practical experience of marketing.

Module One: The Essentials of Marketing

1. **Marketing and the Changing Environment**

   a) **Explain, with an example, how the changing marketing environment is altering the relationship between manufacturers and retailers.**

   ### Introduction

   Tesco has been making a splash about offering premium brands at cut prices. Levi's will not supply Tesco with jeans, arguing that their discounting undermines its brand. Levi's only deal with specialist clothing outlets, who merchandise the jeans properly and charge the full price for them. So Tesco has been sourcing supplies outside the EU, in markets where Levi jeans sell at prices well below those charged in Europe. They then offer them in the UK at £20 less than the high street price.

   To stop them, Levi's took the case to the European Justice's Advocate General in April 2001. The judge's pronouncement was described by an EC spokesperson as 'complex and confusing'. Perhaps this was why both sides claimed victory. Tesco called it a 'key victory for consumers in Britain', whilst Levi's crowed over what it saw as confirmation of 'the existing right of trade mark owners to control imports of their branded products into the European Economic area.' The argument continues.

   ### Body

   This story illustrates a number of points about the changing marketing environment. Starting with the macro-environment (over which companies have little or no control, but which affects their relationships with customers) we can review some STEP factors as follows:

- Socio-Cultural: consumers are attracted by famous clothing brands, as they enjoy the image they can create for themselves.

- Technological: advances in manufacturing have made jeans ever cheaper to produce and copy. This puts pressure on manufacturers to protect their brand images, which cannot be copied.

- Economic: consumers in different countries pay different amounts for the same goods, relative to the local economy. Tesco is taking advantage of this.

- Politico-Legal: the EU presents manufacturers and retailers with a legislative battleground.

A company's micro-environment also affects relationships with customers, but here it has more influence. There are five elements here:

- Suppliers: the balance of power between manufacturers and retailers has shifted almost wholly towards retailer power. Levi's is one of the few suppliers to be holding out.

- Intermediaries: public relations companies and legal firms do well out of such public disputes, as each side tries to make their case.

- Stakeholders: here we can include journalists, for whom the episode provides material to write about.

- Competitors: the case may encourage rival retailers to outdo Tesco's image as the consumer's friend by taking on other brand owners.

- Customers: are becoming more driven by value. At least they are getting cheap jeans.

Conclusion

The tensions between retailers and manufacturers are never going to be resolved. Retailers argue that this is good for consumers because it means lower prices. Manufacturers, however, may be less willing to risk investment in new and improved products if they cannot make sufficient returns.

Sources

Boettcher, D. (2001) 'Tesco claims jeans victory over Levi's', *BBC On-line News,* 5th April. (http://news.bbc.co.uk./hi/english/business/newsid_1261000/1261060.htm)
Kleinman, M. (2001) 'Levi's slams Tesco for "undermining" its brand', *Marketing,* 5th April, p4.

This answer, excluding title and sources, is 447 words long. It demonstrates an understanding of the elements of both the macro and micro levels of the marketing environment, and illustrates each from the story. Use of bullet points helps emphasise the knowledge and understanding displayed in a way that an assessor can recognise quickly.

---

b) **Demonstrate from your own experience how the use of ICT can improve marketing communications.**

Introduction

I take an active part in my children's primary school's Parent Teacher Association. At last month's meeting one of the parents reminded us that the local council had yet to reply to a request we made some time ago about the possibility of moving a nearby zebra crossing to a more convenient place for pedestrians approaching the school. We decided that the best way to get the council to act would be to interest the local newspaper in the issue.

Body

The media are an important stakeholder group in the micro-environment of both school and council. We felt we would benefit from their influence. We also needed a leaflet for all the children to take home to their parents (the school's customers and suppliers in a sense) encouraging them to write to their councillor. I had mentioned to someone before the meeting that I was doing a marketing course, and found myself appointed the campaign's publicity officer.

I have never written a press release or designed a poster before, but learned during the IT skills session at a study centre that word-processing and Desk Top Publishing programmes have templates. These are examples of standard documents that you can adapt. I found a selection of press release templates on the word-processing package, and read the course textbook about how to write an effective press release (Hill & O'Sullivan, 2004, *Foundation Marketing*, (3rd Edition), pp362-366).

I was confident that in sending the result to our local paper that it looked professional and said the right kind of thing. Thinking about the journalist as a customer, I realised I would have to match her expectations of quality for a press release. The template did the trick.

My Desk Top Publishing programme boasted several designs for handbills. I chose one that would look strong in black and white (because it would be reproduced on the school's photocopier). At first I found the type size on the leaflet template was too large to fit in all the words I wanted to include. I reduced the size of the type using the appropriate commands on the computer, but the leaflet lost impact. Clearly the computer template I was following was based on experience of successful design aimed at attracting Attention, stimulating Interest, arousing Desire and prompting Action. I therefore cut the words to the minimum necessary to give the parents some suggested points for their letters, the Town Hall address and names of the relevant councillors.

Conclusions

We appeared on page three of the paper, and letters stimulated by the leaflet have resulted in the school being rung by the Highways Department to arrange an urgent meeting.

Sources

Hill, E. & O'Sullivan, T. (2004) *Foundation Marketing,* (3rd Edition), FT/Prentice Hall.

This answer is 443 words long, excluding title and sources. It illustrates a simple but effective harnessing of Information and Communication Technology towards a specific marketing purpose. Computers in general, and templates in particular, are capable of saving a great deal of time and giving communication materials a professional look. Coverage of issues from marketing and the changing environment is less complete, but there is clear understanding of the concept of stakeholders as part of the micro-environment.

2. Understanding Customers

a) **Illustrate how an understanding of the consumer decision-making process can contribute to the effectiveness of a marketing campaign.**

Introduction

A recent campaign by Lever Faberge, who market the "Dove" brand of toiletries, involved a door-drop campaign in which a free sample of a deodorant was delivered with the morning post, together with a discount voucher for the product worth 30p. The purpose of the campaign was firstly to encourage consumers to try the brand, then to persuade them to switch from their regular brand.

Body

This is an effective approach for several reasons:

1. It works at two key stages in the decision-making process. Firstly **evaluation of alternatives**. The free sample enables consumers to try the product and compare it with their existing brand, without the risk of having to pay for it and then not liking it. Secondly **purchase**. The coupon encourages them to act if they like the product.

2. Deodorants are routine purchases for many consumers, and it is difficult for marketers of fast-moving consumer goods to break peoples' buying habits. This campaign encourages them to think of deodorant as a familiar, but not necessarily routine purchase.

3. The target market for this product is probably a combination of demographic and behavioural segments – namely females who seek the benefit of being able to moisturise their skin when using toiletry products. This is a very broad target market, which is difficult to reach other than by using mass communications, so a door drop is a good way of getting to them. The sample is particularly valuable, as it enables them to experience the benefits themselves.

To investigate the product further, I used a search engine on the Internet to find out more. However, it was not clear which web site would be most useful. My first attempt took me to a site giving details of Unilever's animal rights policies, the second to an online toiletries retailer. This gave details of the product's purpose (but not its benefits), its ingredients and a warning not to use it on broken skin. It was priced at £1.39 (more than I pay for my current brand), but had no mechanism for redeeming my coupon. This all cast doubt on whether it would be worth changing brands.

Conclusion

In conclusion, whilst the Dove promotion effectively influenced some parts of my decision-making process, I did not actually buy the product because my information search and the coupon redemption (the purchase itself) proved problematic. This highlights the importance of implementing marketing campaigns that influence every stage of the decision-making process.

Sources

http://pharmacy2u.co.uk
Nick Pandya, (1999) 'Soft selling soap brings hard profit', *The Guardian,* 2nd October.

This answer is 408 words long, excluding title and sources. It demonstrates an understanding of the consumer decision-making process; an ability to identify a market segment; an appreciation of the process of methods for targeting a chosen market segment; and a competence in accessing the Internet through a search engine.

b) Explain how the concept of the Decision-Making Unit can be used to improve an organisation's marketing.

Introduction

I teach at a college that is part of a large university. Open Days are a very important part of our student recruitment strategy. We have doubled the number we are holding this year in order to give more students and their families a chance to attend.

This extra effort deserves a touch of marketing to make it more effective. The theory of the Decision-Making Unit states that a number of roles are involved in a purchase like choosing a college. 'Marketers must identify the relevant buying roles for their products and services so that they can send appropriate messages to the different members of the DMU, according to their input into the purchasing decision.' (Hill & O'Sullivan).

Were we doing everything we could to reflect this in our Open Day programme?

Body

I listed the DMU roles on a flipchart at a departmental meeting and we discussed how they might relate to the decision to choose a college. I wrote up the chart afterwards.

Initiator: applicant (decides to consider a degree course).

Influencer: sixth-form college or school, parents, friends (provide advice, share experience, discuss).

Decider: applicant (at the end of the day, it's his or her decision).

Buyer: parent (with financial support), applicant (with time and other resources).

User: applicant (needs to feel comfortable).

We felt the "buyer" role was particularly interesting. The applicant is buying us with their time and enthusiasm – and I've always seen them as the "customer". But clearly parents are buying us with financial support for their children. They are both essential, but their motives are different.

As a result of this reflection we have now changed the format of the Open Day. Previously we lumped everyone in together for most of the sessions, dividing applicants by their subject choice. Apart from the opportunity to ask questions, there was little focus on parents. The new format features an afternoon workshop for parents, with short presentations from our financial department and our careers advisors. They cover the economics of student support and graduate recruitment prospects. Meanwhile, applicants are taken in small groups by student guides to see the social and sports facilities of the college, and to take part in interactive quizzes in the IT suite.

Conclusion

It's too early to say whether this more focused approach has increased the proportion of applicants who choose the college, but our feedback sheets from the day have demonstrated a sharp increase in approval ratings from parents.

Sources

Hill, E. & O'Sullivan, T. (2004) *Foundation Marketing,* (3rd Edition), FT/Prentice Hall.

At 410 words this answer manages to convey a sense both of understanding a basic marketing concept in the area of Understanding Customers, and of applying it to a practical problem (increasing the effectiveness of promotional activity). There is at least interim evidence of the problem being solved from the feedback questionnaires, although increased conversion of Open Day attendees to student recruits will be the eventual proof. The quotation is relevant and displays reading, but a summary can often save words. The structure is reasonably logical, but the answer might be improved by using more marketing terminology in order to demonstrate even more understanding (e.g. the treatment of parents and applicants could be seen as moving from mass marketing to target marketing, or the importance of evaluation could be underlined at the end of the piece).

Module Two: The Application of Marketing

1. The Tools of Marketing

a) From your experience as a customer, describe a situation where marketing activity could be performed more effectively and make at least one realistic suggestion for improvement.

Introduction

Recently IKEA's Chief Executive, Anders Dahlvig, admitted that the highly successful furniture retailer's standards of customer service are appalling. Three elements of its marketing mix (product, price and promotion) are so attractive that customers are prepared to tolerate its shortcomings in the fourth: place (or distribution), which is where customer service counts. Shopping at IKEA is exhausting. The stores are unpleasantly crowded at peak times, customers have to walk miles, there can be car parking problems, staff are difficult to find, and what you want is frequently out of stock.

Body

IKEA's problems are all to do with the fourth P – "place", or distribution. They can all be solved, at a price. IKEA should think seriously about changing its approach for a number of reasons. First, customers are notoriously fickle. If a competitor were to match IKEA's performance in the other areas of the marketing mix, and exceed its service standards, the Swedish firm would face severe problems. Part of the problem is simply the number of different items sold. It is surprising, given the basic common sense of market segmentation and targeting, that IKEA does not face more effective competition from firms concentrating on particular types of furniture (office, bedroom or kitchen for example) at budget prices.

Secondly, an effective marketing mix usually has a strong showing from each of the four Ps. A good product for example, helps with promotion, by providing a compelling message of quality. Poor service causes disappointment. After all, what good are low prices if the goods are unavailable?

Finally, customers with money to spend are usually short of time. By increasing its prices and investing the extra profits in customer service, IKEA may find that it is responding to genuine customer needs for convenience, rather than imagined needs for rock-bottom prices.

Conclusion

What forms might such improved customer service take? Here is a list, compiled as a result of a recent visit to IKEA on Junction 27 of the M62 in Yorkshire.

- Car parking attendants.
- More staff in specialist areas.
- Specialist zones for kitchens, bathrooms, bedrooms and office furniture, past which general shoppers can be routed.
- Reduced inventory to ensure higher levels of available stock.
- More effective publicity for the store's Internet-based availability information.
- A premium-rate telephone helpline where goods can be ordered and reserved in advance to prevent arriving at the store and finding they are out of stock.

Sources

Kellaway, L. (2001) 'What a load of rubbish', *Financial Times,* 5th February, p15.
http://www.ikea.com
Personal visit to IKEA, 9th February 2001.

This answer, including title and sources, is 415 words long. It demonstrates an understanding of the marketing mix as applied to a familiar company and, in particular, shows an understanding of the importance of effective distribution. It answers the question relevantly by discussing the problem of poor customer service in the area of distribution and suggests a number of feasible solutions. Finally, it is clearly structured and well laid out, with sources indicated at the end.

---

b) **What are the main challenges to an organisation in pricing either a product or a service?**

Introduction

I spend a good deal of my spare time working as a fund-raising volunteer for my local hospice. This involves trying to come up with fresh and effective ways of making money which will appeal to local people in order to gain their support, and will actually deliver the goods in terms of income for the charity. Good pricing can make all the difference.

Body

The marketing mix is a good way of thinking about fund-raising events. We are always trying to come up with the right idea (product), make it as convenient as possible for people to support it (place), make sure people know about it and are attracted to it (promotion), and charge enough to make a good return for the charity without putting supporters off by being too expensive (price).

Car boot sales seemed to be popular with other charities, but we had never had one. I contacted our local supermarket to see if we could use their car park on a Sunday in June. They have started opening at midday on Sundays now, so they were only able to let us have it until 11am. However, they did not charge us anything, and we were happy to start at 8am. After all, the early bird...

I needed to publicise the event. I worked out that we would have to pay £80 for 200 posters to display through our network of local supporters. The hospice insists that any fund-raising event involving members of the public is adequately insured, so that came to another £50. Luckily we had signs and bunting left over from another event, but we still needed to equip our volunteer stewards with fluorescent vests so that they could be easily identified. The estimated cost of the event, including a margin for surprises, totalled £200.

I knew we had 60 parking spaces available for people selling goods. Using the concept of break-even analysis, I could work out that we would need to charge at least £3.33 for each parking space to cover our costs. But how much would our customers be prepared to pay? I knew that the last car boot sale at the supermarket had charged £6 a space to sellers. But that had been a year ago. Perhaps we could get away with more for the hospice? I knew, too, that there was no other local competition that morning – as I had not seen any publicity for any other car boot sales.

Conclusion

In the end we charged £7 to sellers, and were full a good half hour before the sale opened to the public at 8am. We also decided to charge buyers 50p admission per car, which meant that the sellers felt they were getting serious customers rather than people who were "just looking". My fund-raising committee were so pleased with the financial results that we are thinking of making car boot sales a regular part of our fund-raising. Perhaps we will be able to charge even more next time!

Sources

Hill, E. & O'Sullivan, T. (2004) *Foundation Marketing,* (3rd Edition), FT/Prentice Hall.

This assignment weighs in at 499 words. It could be a bit shorter by being less "chatty" and focusing more on pricing concepts rather than the car boot sale. However, it covers the three main influences of pricing decisions of costs, customers and competition. It could say a bit more about the challenges of pricing a service like a car boot sale. For example, how did the people paying for a parking space from which to sell goods calculate whether they would get

> value for money? The example of the application of the marketing mix to fund-raising events is interesting and relevant not only to Tools of Marketing but to Marketing in Context.

2. Marketing in Context

a) Explain the marketing approach of a non-profit organisation of which you are a customer.

Introduction

My local theatre, the West Oakshire Playhouse (WOP), would be bankrupt within a couple of months if it wasn't subsidised by public money – but its marketing is second to none.

Like all non-profit organisations, WOP exists not to make a return for owners or shareholders, but to fulfil a clearly defined mission – in this case artistic and social.

Body

To understand how and why it does its marketing, let us review its use of the traditional seven Ps of the services marketing mix.

Product: live drama, which can be anything from Shakespeare to the latest offerings from Oakshire's own up-and-coming playwrights. The benefits for audiences are entertainment, excitement and the occasional surprise. The product range deliberately reflects the cultural diversity of Oakshire, so that everyone feels he or she has a stake in the theatre.

Place: all performances happen in the theatre itself, but their times are designed to attract a range of audiences. Midweek matinees at 2pm are popular with the retired population, who appreciate being able get home again before dark. By contrast, weekend late night shows draw an audience of young clubbers. The theatre is easily accessible by public transport and has an underground car park.

Price: while the best seats in the house are expensive enough to attract people who enjoy conspicuous consumption, the majority are well within the budget of most Oakshire residents. There are attractive discounts for students and the unemployed on less popular nights. This brings in marginal sales of seats that might otherwise be empty, as well as widening the audience.

Promotion: posters, leaflets, mailings, listings and press relations are the mainstays of WOP's marketing communication. These reach a wide local audience cost-effectively. The Box Office offers expert advice on choice of performance and seating. The theatre has also invested in telephone sales training for its staff, with pleasing results in terms of income and customer satisfaction. Its web site also has on-line ticket sales.

People: although the front-of-house staff never appear on stage, they are themselves star performers, putting the audience at ease and offering speedy bar and restaurant service when time is of the essence.

Process: car park reservation, ticket collection and a pre-ordered drinks service, are three aspects of the convenient process that guarantees customers stress-free entertainment.

Physical Evidence: some original 1970s features now need updating. But the seats are comfortable, the sight lines in the auditorium are clear, and the bar area has a cosy ambience, with its collection of signed photographs from great thespians who have graced the WOP stage over the years.

Conclusion

Even though it is a non-profit organisation, the WOP uses the same basic marketing approach to reach its audiences as a commercial service company such as a bank or hotel uses to reach its customers.

Sources

West Oakshire Playhouse (2001) 'Annual Report 2000'.
Interview with Julian Woolsack, Marketing Manager WOP, 2nd February 2001.

468 words excluding the title and bibliography. This is a thorough description of the seven Ps of service marketing, as used by an arts organisation in the non-profit sector. It has a clear layout that demonstrates an understanding of the seven Ps model, and some imaginative examples that are always relevant to the stated mission underlying the organisation's marketing. It could be improved by lengthening the conclusion, which would mean a little less detail earlier on to free up available words.

b) **Identify an organisation that supplies goods and services to your organisation, and explain the key marketing issues it faces doing this.**

Introduction

Arts Professional magazine is a trade magazine published fortnightly by my company, Arts Intelligence Ltd. Our biggest supplier is Montague Printers, who prepare the magazine for print; put the ink on the paper; trim, staple and box the finished magazines; and deliver them to a mailing house ready for despatch. As a business-to-business supplier they face a number of key marketing issues.

Body

Product/service: Printers have problems differentiating their services from their competitors, as sophisticated technology means that most printers provide similar levels of print quality. Instead, they have to compete on keeping their customers happy through superior service. When we started looking for a printer, physical evidence was important when we evaluated the alternatives. We looked at samples of work produced for other clients, and visited their premises to see whether they kept a clean and orderly print shop. We also assessed the equipment they had. Because we promise our customers (advertisers and subscribers) that we will deliver their magazines to them on alternate Mondays, our printers have to be 100% reliable. Their processes must be watertight, with effective back-up arrangements for when things go wrong. Their people are important too. We have to be confident that their staff will communicate efficiently and always be ready to print our job at the agreed time.

Pricing: printing is a highly competitive industry, where undercutting other printers is a common way to attract new business. Montague's gained our business because they were the cheapest supplier who could meet our production schedule. They would like to increase their prices to cover their rising costs. However, other printers have offered us even cheaper prices, and although Montague's quality of service is very good, we do not believe it is worth the additional £300 an issue above the levels of other printers. Montague's will have to decide whether to meet the price levels of their competitors or risk losing it altogether.

Promotion: Such is the importance of interpersonal communications in the printing process that personal selling is the most vital form of promotion. Whenever we require additional printed matter, such as our advertising rate cards or our annual wallplanner, we approach Montague's for a quote. We also approach other printers, and select these based on word-of-mouth recommendations. We do not respond to advertising or direct mail from unknown suppliers. We feel we need some level of confidence in a supplier before using them.

Place: the growth of electronic communications has meant that printers' clients no longer need to be located physically close to their printers to receive a good service. This is a threat to Montague's as its local customers, such as ourselves, now have more printers to choose from who can meet tight production schedules. This increase in choice has fuelled competition and forced price levels down.

Conclusion

This report demonstrates the way in which the marketing mix of four Ps, with three additional Ps for service marketing, is used in the competitive world of business-to-business marketing.

Sources

Montague Printers (2003) Annual Report.
Hill, E. & O'Sullivan, T. (2004) *Foundation Marketing*, (3rd Edition), FT/Prentice Hall.

At 496 words this report is just inside the limit. It is well written and clear, and demonstrates a sound understanding of the issues faced by a business-to-business supplier in a competitive market, structured along the lines of the marketing mix. It also gives an insight into what business customers are looking for from their suppliers. While it would have to reduce the number of words elsewhere in the report, the conclusion could say a little more about how the business-to-business marketing mix here is different from a typical consumer mix (for example the increased importance of personal selling as a promotional technique).

REPORT WRITING

There is no such thing as a "template" for writing a report on a marketing theme. Rather, a report should reflect the task it is required to deliver. So a useful checklist to consider is:

Content

Prepare an outline of your work, which might include:

- **Introduction** – an explanation as to what you are writing about, and a little background to the issue you will be exploring.

- **Body** – clearly defined sections, each of which cover a theme that you want to explore, and links it to the relevant marketing theories. Make use of bullet points and even subheadings to highlight the key points you are trying to convey.

- **Conclusions** – having explored the issues, what is your opinion in relation to the question you are answering.

- **Appendix** – this should always include material that relates to the report, but is not integral to understanding the content of it. In the case of this assignment, you are asked to list the resources that have informed your report.

Language

Express yourself clearly and concisely, and wherever appropriate, use the relevant marketing terminology. Read through your own work afterwards to ensure that your sentences are well constructed, and your grammar and spelling are accurate.

Length

The length of this report is given to you, which makes life simple! If your work is too short, you risk not covering some of the key material relating to the issues you are exploring. However, if it is too long, you will undoubtedly include detail that is unnecessary and that might complicate your arguments.

Layout

Good layout should make it easier for the reader to follow what you are trying to say. Fancy design gimmicks and multiple fonts are not necessary, and can be distracting. But a consistent layout, which makes limited use of bold, underline, capitals or italics when appropriate can be helpful. All reports should be word processed, unless there are technical reasons why this is not possible.

Graphics

Clear diagrams or charts can be extremely helpful in explaining concepts that are difficult to convey in words, but ensure that your graphics are clearly drawn, and just as important, clearly labelled.

MAKING A PRESENTATION

The prospect of making a presentation is probably something that strikes terror into the heart of most people, so if you are nervous about the thought of standing up and telling an assembled gathering about your research or project then join the club! There are two pretty useful ways of dealing with the fear of making a presentation, most of which relates to fear of the unknown. Firstly, do it a lot, as practise not only makes perfect, it also builds confidence. A more immediate solution though is preparation, which is another way of reducing the unknown. In preparation, you should really study the material you want to present, so that you feel you know what you are talking about. You should then consider the full range of elements that comprise a good presentation.

Content

Before you get going with your preparation, decide what you want to say and who you will be saying it to. Understanding the objectives of the presentation is key to designing an appropriate format and a persuasive argument.

The Start

Think about how you will introduce yourself and what you are planning to do in the presentation. Listeners also appreciate a "route map" that tells them what you are planning to communicate.

Delivery Technique

A warm smile and engagement with the audience through eye contact is one of the most valuable ways of getting people on your side – though admittedly difficult to achieve when you're extremely nervous. Even if you can't quite manage this, then attempt to avoid the common pitfalls: mumbling, hesitancy (..."er"...), gabbling, catch phrases (... "you know what I mean"...), mannerisms and gazing at the floor.

Visuals

Such is the effectiveness of presentation software such as Microsoft PowerPoint, that even if you are incredibly nervous, it is possible to present amazing visual aids which you can prepare in advance and which will help you win the day! Good slides have real impact. You may wish to put words on them, but not too many, not too small, and not at a funny angle. Always present diagrams rather than tables of figures, which are difficult to follow on a screen.

Summary

Because you will probably have included a range of quite detailed material, it is useful to summarise the key points you have made, to reinforce them and draw your presentation together at the end. This sets the scene for inviting questions from the audience.

Questions

Audiences ask questions for many reasons, only some of which are because they want to find out more about your work. Sometimes people disagree with what you have said, and want their own views to be heard. Others may want to show off how knowledgeable they are. Your role is simply to respond, so provided you are confident that you know what you're talking about, you can sit back and relax at this stage!

Appendix 3

Answers to multiple-choice questions

Session 1	Session 2	Session 3	Session 4	Session 5	Session 6
1. b	1. a and b	1. c	1. b	1. c	1. d
2. b	2. b	2. c and d	2. c	2. c and d	2. a and c
3. a	3. d	3. c	3. a and c	3. c	3. c
4. b	4. c	4. d	4. d	4. a	4. d
5. b	5. d	5. a and c	5. b	5. b	5. a and b
Session 7	**Session 8**	**Session 9**	**Session 10**	**Session 11**	**Session 12**
1. d	1. a	1. a	1. c	1. a	1. c
2. d	2. b	2. b	2. d	2. b	2. c
3. b	3. d	3. c	3. c	3. c	3. a
4. b	4. b	4. a	4. b	4. b	4. a
5. b	5. a	5. c	5. a	5. c	5. c

Appendix 4

Syllabus detail

This guide gives you details of the chapter and page references of Hill and O'Sullivan's *Foundation Marketing* 3rd Edition that deal with the syllabus topics of the CIM Introductory Certificate in Marketing. We hope it will be of use to both tutors and students in guiding their reading and revision.

Topic	Reference **Chapter** and pages e.g. **1**, 11-13
Module One: The Essentials of Marketing	
Marketing and the changing environment	
Marketing and its importance to the organisation	
■ Definitions of marketing	**1**, 2-7, 17, 45
■ Marketing orientation and its alternatives	**1**, 10, 11, 14-16
■ The marketing concept and its implementation	**1**, 16-21
■ Reasons for the growth of marketing	**1**, 8-13
■ Future directions for marketing: societal marketing; relationship marketing	**1**, 7, 26 **3**, 70
Planning for marketing activity	
■ Marketing Audit	**3**, 60-83 **14**, 403-422
■ SWOT analysis	**14**, 411-413
■ Marketing objectives	**14**, 417-418
■ Marketing strategies and tactics	**1**, 18, 20 **14**, 402-422
■ Marketing budgets	**11**, 308-309 **14**, 411-422

■ Product life cycles	**7**, 189-197 **8**, 225, 242 **13**, 374, 388.
■ Brands	**7**, 196, 199-205
Price	
■ Pricing for profit (price skimming, premium pricing, differential pricing, auctions)	**9**, 242-244
■ Pricing for volume (penetration pricing, discounting)	**9**, 244-247
■ Cost influences on price (fixed and variable costs: break-even analysis)	**9**, 251-253
■ Customer influences on price (price sensitivity, price elasticity)	**9**, 238, 256-258
■ Competitor influences on price	**9**, 256-258
Place	
■ Marketing channels: types of intermediary	**10**, 266-274
■ Functions of agents, merchants, wholesalers and retailers	**10**, 272-274, 282-289
■ Channel choice: selective, intensive and exclusive distribution	**10**, 280
■ E-commerce and distribution	**10**, 280-282
■ Physical distribution (order processing, materials handling, warehousing, inventory management and transport)	**10**, 289-293

Promotion	
■ AIDA model of marketing communication	**11**, 303 **12**, 339-340
■ Push and Pull strategies	**10**, 271, 280 **12**, 355-356
■ Uses, advantages and limitations of Advertising	**11**, 305-320
■ Uses, advantages and limitations of Editorial PR	**12**, 358-369
■ Uses, advantages and limitations of Sales Promotion	**12**, 349-358
■ Uses, advantages and limitations of Selling	**12**, 336-348
■ Uses, advantages and limitations of Internet (web sites; internet advertising)	**12**, 320-322
Marketing in context	
■ Services marketing (differences between products and services; characteristics of service provision)	**1**, 22 **2**,33-38 **9**, 240, 242 **10**, 293-295
■ Not-for-Profit marketing (differences from commercial marketing in terms of objectives and operational approaches)	**2**, 24, 31, 45-50
■ International marketing (reasons for going international; market entry methods and barriers)	**13**, 373-378, 381-395.
■ Business-to-business marketing (differences from consumer emphases in marketing mix)	**2**, 39-44 **10**, 281, 284

Index

Remember that there are definitions of key terms at the end of each Session.

statistics.gov.uk 24
STEP factors 23-28, 203
straight rebuy 206
strategies versus tactics 12
subsistence economy 10
Sunny Delight 84-5
suppliers 30
supply chains 11
surveys 56, 59-64
SWOT analysis 12

Target Group Index 46
target marketing 90-103
technological factors 25
telephone surveys 60
Tesco 16, 225-7
theatre-goers 97-8
Thomas Cook 135
Thomson 134-5
toothpaste 97
trade associations 46
transport 149
tweens 95

umbrella branding 186
undifferentiated marketing 90-1
unfamiliar processes 83
Unique Selling Proposition (USP)
108
usage rate 97
user 79
user expertise 97
USP (Unique selling proposition) 108

variable costs 128-9, 132-3

WAP technology (wireless
application protocol) 34-5, 171
warehousing 148, 151
web site surveys 60
web sites 10, 25, 44, 47-9, 147, 168-

70 see also Internet
Webvan 152-3
wholesalers 142-3

Yakult 101

Notes

WEST CHESHIRE COLLEGE

LIBRARY & LEARNING RESOURCES